Who was Sitting Bull? • What makes rainbows appear? • **What is virtual reality?**

How do you travel light? • Who were the Maya? • **What's at the center of Earth?**

Who was Mozart? • Is a four-leaf clover lucky? • **Why do monkeys groom each other?**

Do vampires really exist? • What are robots used for? • **Do animals use tools?**

What causes twins? • **Who was Harry Houdini?** • Are all sharks dangerous?

Who was Jackie Robinson? • **What is a meteor?** • Who was Queen Elizabeth I?

How do plants eat? • **How do spiders spin webs?** • What is a vaccine?

When was the first car invented? • **How does an electric guitar work?**

BIGGEST BOOK OF QUESTIONS & ANSWERS

Text by
Jane Parker Resnick
Rebecca L. Grambo
& Tony Tallarico

Illustrations by
Tony Tallarico

Kidsbooks®

Visit us at **www.kidsbooks.com**®

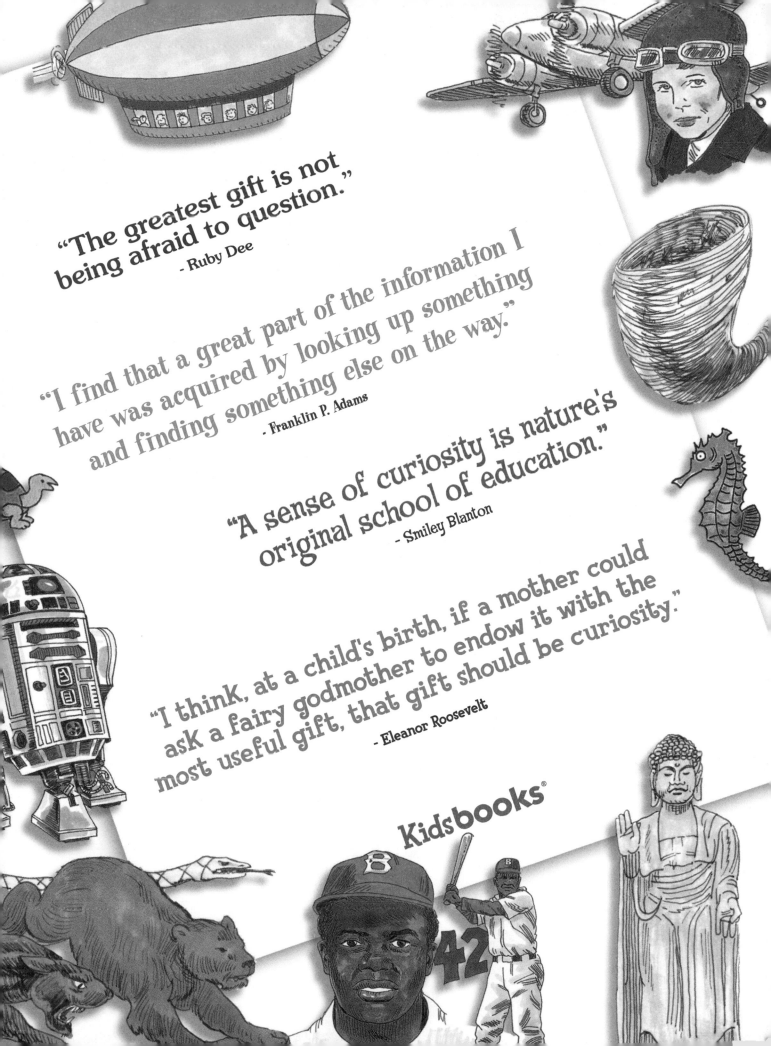

"The greatest gift is not being afraid to question."
– Ruby Dee

"I find that a great part of the information I have was acquired by looking up something and finding something else on the way."
– Franklin P. Adams

"A sense of curiosity is nature's original school of education."
– Smiley Blanton

"I think, at a child's birth, if a mother could ask a fairy godmother to endow it with the most useful gift, that gift should be curiosity."
– Eleanor Roosevelt

Kidsbooks®

How many people live in the world?

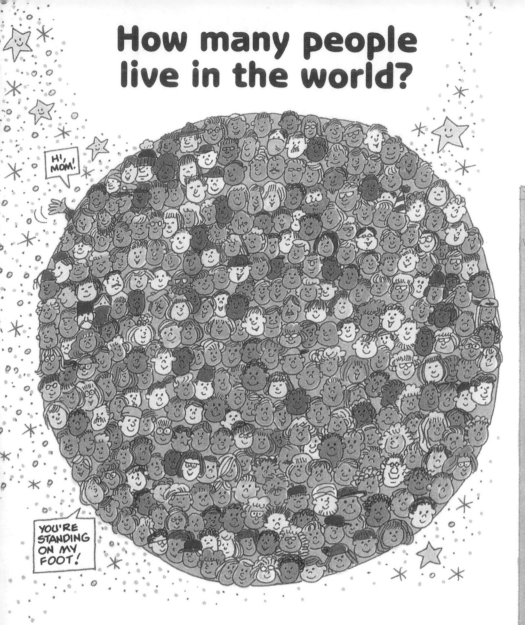

At the end of 2007, the population of the world was believed to be more than 6.6 billion. By 2020, scientists estimate that eight billion people will inhabit Earth and by 2030 that number could grow to over nine billion.

What is the difference between a sea and an ocean?

Seas are smaller than oceans. A sea can be part of one of the four oceans (Atlantic, Pacific, Indian, and Arctic). The Caribbean Sea of North America, for instance, is in the Atlantic. Other seas, such as the Caspian Sea in Asia, are surrounded by land.

How tall is the world's tallest living tree?

A giant redwood in California's Redwood National Park is the tallest tree on Earth. How tall is it? You could look out the top-floor window of a building 35 stories high—and still not see the top. Discovered in the summer of 2006, the tree, named Hyperion, is a whopping 379.1 feet tall!

What makes a skunk smell?

That ghastly spray is the skunk's best defense and, boy, does it work! No creature, human or beast, can stand being near a skunk with that odor. It comes from a fluid called musk, which is produced and stored in a pair of glands under the animal's tail. A skunk can propel its spray about 10 feet!

When were comic books invented?

Comic books are single-square newspaper cartoons that have grown up. From single-square cartoons came comic strips, which are several squares long. The first comic book as we know it was *Funnies on Parade*, a one-time publication that came out in 1933. The first comic-book series was Famous Funnies, which first appeared in 1934. The first comic-book superhero, Superman, landed on newsstands in 1939.

What is the Loch Ness Monster?

Now you see it, now you don't! In 1933, a couple claimed they saw a dinosaur-like monster in Loch Ness, a lake in Scotland. Three thousand sightings of "Nessie" have occurred since, but none of them has proven the creature's existence for sure!

Why do people snore?

If someone catches you snoring, blame your uvula (OOV-you-la). It's a small piece of flesh at the back of the throat that hangs down from the roof of the mouth. Sometimes air from the lungs causes the uvula to vibrate—and that's the snoring sound. It happens most often when you breathe through your mouth.

What is a jet stream?

Jet streams are Earth's fastest large-scale winds. A large-scale wind is a high current of air that blows over vast distances. About 30,000 to 35,000 feet above Earth's surface, large masses of cold air move in from the poles to clash with warmer air masses from the tropics. This creates the mighty rivers of wind known as jet streams.

Why are feet so ticklish?

HA·HA!
HEE·HEE!
HO·HO!

Nerve endings are what make us feel ticklish. And the more nerve endings there are in a particular spot, the more ticklish it is. Our feet have the most nerve endings—so they're the most ticklish of all!

How big is the biggest diamond in the world?

Diamonds, like other gems, are measured in carats. (Not carrots, those are for rabbits.) A carat weighs 0.2 grams. The largest fine quality, colorless diamond ever found was called "The Cullinan." It was mined in South Africa and weighed 3,106 carats. It was cut into 106 jewels and produced the finest, largest gemstone ever, weighing 530.2 carats.

11

What is octopus ink?

It's a smoke screen. When threatened, an octopus discharges a thick blackish or brownish inky fluid that is stored in its body. The ejected ink doesn't dissolve quickly. It floats in the water in a cloud shaped somewhat like an octopus. The idea is to confuse its enemies and cover its escape—and it works.

Who invented *pizza?*

Pizza was first cooked up in the kitchens of Naples, Italy, about 500 years ago. No one person created it. It was just something a lot of people ate around Naples. The Duke of Naples made pizza popular by adding a variety of toppings. Without cheese and tomato sauce toppings, pizza is just plain crusty dough.

Why can't I see in the dark?

The human eye uses light to see. Light bounces off your surroundings and into your eye through your pupil, the black hole at the center. A picture forms on your retina, the lining at the back of the eye. Your brain makes sense out of what you see. Without light, there is nothing to enter your retina and start the whole process going.

What is ESP?

ESP stands for Extra Sensory Perception. Regular sensory perception is the way we experience the world through our five senses—sight, hearing, smell, taste, and touch. But "extra" goes beyond that and includes having an awareness of information NOT gained through the senses. That could include having dreams that come true, hearing the voices of dead people, or getting a strong feeling about something that is going to happen in the future.

Why is it considered unlucky to open an umbrella indoors?

Umbrellas were first used by African royalty to shield themselves from the hot rays of the sun god. To open one in the shade insulted the god. To open one indoors must have been worse, probably punishable by the god. Today, we think of it as just plain unlucky.

HOW DO CLOUDS FORM?

Millions of water droplets together form clouds. They start out as *water vapor*, the evaporated water that rises from lakes, oceans, rivers, and plants. Water vapor cools as it rises into the air and, as the temperature drops, it changes to liquid. These masses of tiny water droplets form clouds. When the clouds get too heavy, they fall to Earth as rain. The rain flows into lakes and rivers...and the whole process begins all over again.

HOW MANY INVENTIONS DID THOMAS EDISON INVENT?

Almost 1100! The great American inventor Thomas Edison made and patented an enormous number of inventions. Among them, he invented an early version of a movie projector that linked movies with sound. But he is best known for inventing the phonograph, and for figuring out a way to make and mass produce the long-lasting incandescent light bulb. Edison first publicly demonstrated his light bulb in 1879—and in 1882 the first commercial electric power station was born!

WHAT IS STONEHENGE?

Stonehenge is a mystery—on a grand scale. An enormous ancient monument, Stonehenge was built in southern England over 3,000 years ago. The monument consists of many large stones, some weighing up to 100,000 pounds, arranged in circular patterns. It may have been used to observe the movements of the sun and moon—and then to create calendars. No one really knows.

Why can I drink something really hot, but if I spilled the same thing on myself, it would burn?

Your mouth has air-conditioning! As you sip a hot liquid, air comes into your mouth along with it and cools the drink. Your saliva mixes in and cools it further. But hot stuff on your skin is just plain hot!

Who wrote the song
"Happy Birthday to You"?

The Hill girls, Mildred and Patty, wrote "Good Morning to You" in 1893. The song was not a big hit until someone changed the words. No one knows exactly who made the change. There aren't many words, but for birthdays, four are all you need:

Happy Birthday to You!

15

What's the difference between a dolphin and a porpoise?

Their facial structure and body size. Both are mammals, not fish, and have to breathe above water. Both are related to whales, but are smaller. Dolphins can grow to 12 feet in length and have a beak. Porpoises are beakless and are usually between three and six feet long.

WE'RE MAMMAL COUSINS,

-46 -47 -48 -49- 50-51 - 52-53 - 54-55-56 -

WHAT'S THE DIFFERENCE BETWEEN AN INSECT AND A SPIDER ?

Look out for legs. Spiders have eight. Insects have six. Also check out the antennae. Insects have them and spiders don't. Up close (if you dare), look at the number of body parts. Insects have three. Spiders have two. And if the animal is hanging by a thread, it's a spider. Spiders make silk. Insects don't.

How fast do a hummingbird's wings beat?

Faster than you can see. Hummingbirds, the smallest feathered creatures on the planet, are also the fastest wing-beaters. The beating is so speedy it looks like a blur. With a slow motion camera, it can almost be counted—50 to 75 beats per second! Hummingbirds can even fly backwards, something no other bird can do.

WHY DO ZEBRAS AND TIGERS HAVE STRIPES?

I'M NOT HERE.

I HOPE YOU CAN'T SEE ME!

Camouflage—to help them hide. If a zebra or a tiger were in your backyard, you'd know it. But if you were in their neighborhood, you might miss them. Striped coats are hard to see in the light and dark shadows of forests and grasslands. This helps to keep them safe from predators. Now you see them. Now you don't!

DO YOU HEAR A RATTLE?

The vibration of shell-like rings on the end of its tail. The rattle is made up of dry, hard pieces of unshed skin. As the snake grows, the number of rings increases. So, the louder the rattle, the bigger the snake. The snake will shake its rattles to tell an intruder to..."Take off!"

What makes a rattlesnake's tail rattle?

I'M GOING OUT!

Why does a match light up?

In a word—friction. Matches were the accidental discovery of John Walker, a chemist. In 1827, he was trying to produce a burnable material for shotguns. His first match was a stick he was using to stir a mixture of chemicals. It burst into flames when he scraped it against a stone floor to clean off the end.

How often can we see an eclipse of the sun?

Solar eclipses can be seen only from certain parts of Earth's surface—different places at different times. If you're willing to travel, however, the average number of eclipses is two to five times a year. Five is highly unusual. The last time Earth experienced five solar eclipses in a year was 1935; it won't happen again until 2206!

When were roller skates invented?

Talk about an entrance! To introduce his invention, Joseph Merlin of Huy, Belgium, roller-skated into a ballroom playing the violin. That was in 1759. Unfortunately, he didn't know how to stop and crashed into a full-length mirror, breaking his violin.

Who invented money?

The first piece of metal to be considered a coin was invented in Lydia, Turkey, around 670 B.C. But the idea of money took shape over a long time. People traded ten chickens for a cow, or a basket of berries for six ears of corn. But what if the person with the berries wanted wheat instead of corn? Or what if the owner of the berries left them at home? Eventually, it made sense to have something that always had the same value and was easy to carry. And that something was money.

WHAT IS GLASS MADE OF?

OOPS!

Glass starts out being soft and syrupy. It's a mixture of sand, soda, and limestone melted together at high temperatures. In this state it can be shaped into the glass objects we see around us. Various minerals can be added to make different colored glass. Then, the "syrup" is cooled, heated, and cooled again in a process that makes it hard.

How many stars are in the Milky Way galaxy?

3,050,043, 3,050,044, 3,050,045, 3,050,046, 3,050,047...

At least 100 billion, including the sun. Those billions of stars are arrayed in a vast spiral that is about 100,000 light-years in diameter. The Milky Way's many stars are constantly moving, rotating around the galaxy's center. How fast is that rotation? Our sun, which is on one of the galaxy's outer arms, takes 200 million to 230 million years to make one complete rotation!

DID HE COUNT US YET?

I'M HEADING FOR THE MILKY WAY!

STOP PUSHING!

THIS IS A GRADE "A" GALAXY.

What makes popcorn pop?

Every kernel of corn has a tiny droplet of water in it. Heat the kernel, and the water turns to steam. Steam takes up more space than water, so it presses against the walls of the kernel. The corn expands and expands and...explodes! Popppppp!

IT MUST HAVE BEEN THE POPCORN!

HIC·HIC·HIC·HIC·HIC·HIC·HIC·HIC·HIC·

STAND CLEAR FOR POPPING POPCORN

IT'S A BLAST!

THANK YOU.

I LIKE POPCORN!

WHY DO I GET THE HICCUPS?

It all starts with your diaphragm, the big muscle below your lungs. Usually, the diaphragm works smoothly, expanding and contracting your lungs. But if it gets irritated, perhaps by eating too quickly, it pulls down sharply. Air whooshes into your lungs...Hic! To keep too much air from entering your lungs, a small flap at the top of your windpipe snaps shut...Cup!

I'M ON A DIET!

What is the most powerful muscle in my body?

Your jaw muscle—and it's because exercise makes muscles stronger! Talking and chewing exercise this muscle more than any other.

WHAT DO INSECTS EAT?

That depends on the insect. Some, such as potato beetles, eat leaves. Termites eat wood. Some insects, including bees, butterflies, and male mosquitoes, suck nectar from flowers. Female mosquitoes suck blood. Many other insects eat other insects. Some, such as water striders, even eat others of their own kind!

How do you make potato chips?

Deep-fat frying is the good old-fashioned way. Slice some potatoes as thinly as possible. Soak them in cold water for two hours, changing the water twice. Drain them and dry them carefully with paper towels. In a deep pot, bring some cooking oil to a high heat. Drop the potato slices into the hot oil. Shake and stir, cooking them until they're golden. Drain them on paper towels and eat. Delicious! If you want to try making your own potato chips, ask an adult for some help!

I BET YOU CAN'T EAT ONLY ONE!

IS THAT MY BEEPER?

How do whales talk?

They sing! Or to be specific, male humpback whales do. The songs of the humpbacks are a form of communication much stronger than the human voice. Underwater, whales send messages heard several miles away. Whales make sounds with a system of tubes and air sacs around their blowholes. Squeaks and whistles and strange moaning are what whale songs sound like to humans. The songs of male humpbacks have been taped. People listen to these recordings as they would any other kind of music.

Why do flamingos stand on one leg?

Standing on one leg and then the other helps a flamingo conserve body heat and energy. It also allows each limb to dry and keep warm.

Do animals use tools?

Some do. The woodpecker finch of the Galapagos Islands uses a tool to dig insects out of holes. The bird uses a cactus spine, which it holds in its beak. Apes use twigs and blades of grass to hunt insects. Seabirds use rocks. They drop clams and other hard-shelled sea creatures against the hard rocks to split open their shells.

HOW DOES AN ELECTRIC GUITAR WORK?

Play an electric guitar and you are actually producing sound with an amplifier and a loudspeaker, not a set of strings. Each metal string is attached to a pick-up, which is a small coil of wire with magnets set in it. The pick-up sends an electrical signal to the amplifier, then to the loudspeaker, and right out to your audience.

What is Silly Putty™?

A substance that bounces, stretches, and picks up ink when pressed against newsprint. Its inventor saw no practical use for the odd stuff, but a businessman named Peter Hodgson recognized its potential as a toy. Hodgson named it Silly Putty and, in 1949, started selling one-ounce balls of it in colorful plastic eggs. It was a great success: Children around the world still play with it today.

What's the difference between a tortoise and a turtle?

A tortoise lives on land. It has clubbed feet like an elephant and a shell that is high-domed and thick. The largest tortoises can be 500 pounds. The turtle is a water creature with legs that resemble flippers. Leatherback turtles, by far the largest turtle, can grow to eight feet and weigh 1,500 pounds!

HOW DO YOU MAKE ANIMATION?

Bugs bunny bites a carrot. Beauty kisses the Beast. The movement looks natural, but it's really made up of hundres of *still* drawings. These drawings are flipped very fast in a row—24 per second! The speed gives the illusion of movement. How are the drawings "flipped"? . . . by using a special high-speed camera. Today, computers are often used to create the still drawings, and they are also used to help make the drawings "move."

How does a caterpillar turn into a butterfly?

It's not a miracle . . . it's *metamorphosis*, which means "change of form." A butterfly begins life as an egg, which grows into a caterpillar. After a period of maturing, a hard shell called a *chrysalis* develops over the caterpillar. Inside, the creature's body gradually changes. The shell breaks open, and out comes a lovely butterfly.

WHAT ARE THE FISH LIKE AT THE BOTTOM OF THE OCEAN?

The deeper you go, the darker it gets. Many fish that live at 2,000 feet or deeper have their own flashlights. They are *luminous*—they glow with light-producing cells. This light helps them get around in the blackness and attract prey. Other fish are blind—since they can't see down there, they never developed functioning eyes. Most of all, it's *cold* at the bottom—sometimes as cold as 28 degrees Fahrenheit. Luckily for the fish that live there, their bodies are adapted to those temperatures and they don't seem to mind!

HI!

What was the first tool?

In the early 1990s, archaeologists found sharp-edged stone fragments in a dry riverbed in Ethiopia in Africa. Much older than earlier finds, these became the oldest known tools made by humans—more than 2.52 million years old! These items would have been handy for digging, scraping, and hacking.

How do evergreens stay green all year?

It's due to the shape of their leaves—or needles. Trees take up water through their roots. The water evaporates into the air through their leaves. Trees with flat, broad leaves lose a lot of water. In winter, when the ground is frozen, these trees shed their leaves to hold on to their water supply. But evergreens have needle-like leaves with a thick, waxy covering. These needles don't lose much moisture, so they remain on the tree. After a few years, they fall off, but new ones grow in at the same time, so the tree is *ever green!*

How can a parrot talk?

I DON'T LIKE CRACKERS!

By repeating the "nonsense" sounds it hears over and over and over again. When a parrot says "Polly wants a cracker," it doesn't have a cracker in mind. The bird can't understand what it's saying. But it can learn to make the sounds by practicing. In the same way, you could learn to say a few sentences in a foreign language you didn't know.

How do bees make honey?

It all starts with nectar, the sugary juice of flowers that honeybees bring back to the hive. In the hive, worker bees add important enzymes (or chemicals) from their bodies to the nectar and deposit it in the honeycombs. Then, special bees fan this nectar with their wings. The heat of the hive and the fanning make some of the water in the nectar evaporate, and turn it into honey.

How does a sprouting seed know which way is up?

WHICH WAY IS UP?

Gravity gives the seed direction. Tiny nodules in the growing tips of seeds respond to gravity so that the roots are pulled downward. That way, the shoots will always point up.

How old is the universe?

Between 13.5 and 14 billion years is the best estimate. The most widely accepted theory for how the universe began is the Big Bang Theory. Astronomers believe that all matter was once a single mass. Then an enormous explosion sent pieces flying off into space, creating galaxies, stars, and planets. The Big Bang theory says that the universe is expanding and that the galaxies are still moving away from each other.

HAPPY BIRTHDAY!!

LOOK AT THAT!!

What is a meteor?

Meteors have more than one name, just like people. Particles of matter or pieces of rock that fall through space are called meteoroids. If they burn up in the Earth's atmosphere, they are called meteors. Most of them burn into nothing and are never seen again, but if they survive and hit the ground, they become meteorites and form big craters where they land.

WHY DO WE SNEEZE?

Your nose knows. Anything that gets in your nose, like dust or germs, is something your body doesn't want. You sneeze to get rid of it. The big A-Choo! is air from your lungs that comes up, shoots rapidly through your nose, and clears it.

A-A-CHOO!

Who was Mozart?

Wolfgang Amadeus Mozart was one of the world's most brilliant musicians. He was born in Austria in 1756 and composed his first piece for a full symphony orchestra at the age of five! He also performed. During his lifetime, he composed many symphonies, concertos, and operas—some of the most beautiful music ever written. And he lived only 35 years.

Why is a four-leaf clover considered lucky?

Legends about the four-leaf clover go all the way back to Adam and Eve. It is said that Eve took a four-leaf clover when she was sent from the Garden of Eden. A piece of green from the world's first garden spot must be something rare and wonderful—special enough to bring good luck.

HOW MANY DIFFERENT KINDS OF BIRDS ARE THERE?

Probably over 9,000. No one knows for sure because many of them live in places where people seldom can see them, such as in the dense rain forest. For this reason, new species are still being discovered in remote areas of the planet. Birds are ancient creatures that probably evolved from dinosaurs, and most species that have lived on the earth are now extinct. Those we know about today come in all varieties: large and small; colorful and plain; tuneful, noisy, and silent. Although all birds have feathers and wings, some, like the penguin and ostrich, can't even fly.

WHO INVENTED NUMBERS?

Numbers are really ideas. We can't see them, so we create signs or symbols to represent them. The concept of numbers, and the symbols to represent them, developed when people needed to count things. Different civilizations used different kinds of numbers. The 1, 2, 3 type of numbers we use are called Arabic numerals. They were probably invented by the Hindus in India about 1,400 years ago. But it isn't the oldest system. The Babylonians invented a number system about 3,500 years ago.

WHAT IS GRAVITY?

The big pull. Gravity is the force at the center of a planet that attracts other objects to it. The Earth's force of gravity keeps our feet on the ground. Gravity actually holds the universe together, too. The sun's gravity keeps the planets in their orbits. Without it, the Earth would shoot off into space.

How do bubbles get in fizzy drinks?

Nature didn't do it. Manufacturers give drinks the fizz that tickles your taste buds. First, they force carbon dioxide into the drink under pressure and seal the bottle or can. The gas stays in the liquid until you open the drink. Then . . . *whoosh! hiss!* . . . the carbon dioxide escapes. Where does it go? It's in the bubbles.

HOW LONG HAVE ESCALATORS BEEN GOING UP AND DOWN?

About a century. Coney Island, New York, had the world's first escalator in 1896. In London in 1911, people were worried about putting their feet on that city's first moving stairs. So a man with a wooden leg was hired to take the ride and show that if a man with one leg could do it, the two-legged types had nothing to fear.

OOPS!

SPEED LIMIT 10 MPH

HOW DOES A FLYING FISH FLY?

Not like a bird. These small fish (the largest is about a foot and a half) propel themselves into the air with their tails and glide. Fear makes them do it. If a bigger fish is chasing them, they flap their tails, pick up speed, and leap out of the water. Then they spread their front fins and sail on the breeze—up to 20 miles per hour.

What happens when I dream?

You "see" your dreams with your eyes. Dream sleep is called REM sleep for Rapid Eye Movement because your eyes move behind your closed lids as if you were scanning a picture. Scientists think that dreaming is a way of sorting out and storing the happenings of the day.

Who invented indoor plumbing?

Someone we should all thank. On the Mediterranean island of Crete, a system was installed 4,000 years ago. Indoor plumbing requires pipes that bring water into the house and drainage pipes that take waste out. The flush toilet was invented by Sir John Harrington in 1589, but didn't reach its present form until the 1800s.

What is QUICKSAND?

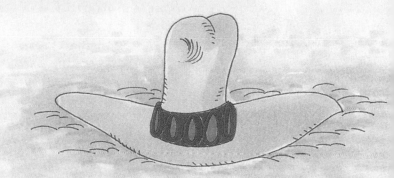

A very thick liquid that is formed when water flows through and mixes with sand. Quicksand appears to be firm enough to walk on, but any object that steps into or lands on the soft mixture will sink into it. You can't "stand" vertically in water and expect to keep your head above it. The same is true of quicksand.

What makes the Leaning Tower of Pisa lean?

The Leaning Tower of Pisa in northern Italy is a church bell tower. Its construction began in 1173, but was soon halted when the builders realized the 10-foot foundation wasn't deep enough to keep the tower from tilting in the soft soil. The 180-foot tower, weighing 16,000 tons, was finally completed 200 years later. To keep it from toppling over, the people of Pisa have repeatedly gone in and reinforced the foundation. But they haven't dared try to straighten the tower!

EVERYBODY— PULL TOGETHER!

UGH!

OOFF!

IT'S NOT MOVING

Why do people have straight, wavy, or curly hair?

As a strand of hair grows, it squeezes through a tiny hole called a follicle. The shape of a person's follicles makes hair straight, wavy, or curly. Think of a toothpaste tube—if the opening weren't round, but shaped like a square or a star instead, the stream of toothpaste would look completely different. Straight hair grows out of round follicles, waves from oval follicles, and tight, round curls spring from square follicles!

Why do salmon and other fish swim upstream?

THIS WAY

Because they return to where they were born when they are ready to breed. And that can be a long way—sometimes thousands of miles. Salmon are born in rivers and streams and then travel to sea to live as adults. But instinct helps them find their way home. They swim against the current and even jump over waterfalls trying to find the exact spot where they were born.

What causes EARTHQUAKES?

THIS IS A GOOD TIME TO MAKE A MILKSHAKE!

The problem is underground. Pressure inside the Earth causes giant plates of rocks in the Earth's crust to shove against one another. When these rock plates collide, the Earth's surface cracks, and the ground shakes. The shock waves carry the shudders for miles, and the Earth *quakes*.

Who started April Fool's Day?

Silly days for practical jokes are found all around the world. Perhaps the day started with the French, who once began the new year on the first of April. In 1564, when the new calendar began the year with January 1, some people resisted. They were considered April fools.

What was the first movie?

In Paris, France, in 1895, Louis and Auguste Lumiere showed the first moving picture, a short film of workers leaving a factory. The first movie with a story was Edwin Porter's *The Great Train Robbery* in 1903. It was a sensation, but silent. In 1927, *The Jazz Singer* was the first full-length movie with sound.

TODAY, THE TRAIN WOULD BE LATE !!

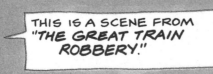

THIS IS A SCENE FROM "THE GREAT TRAIN ROBBERY."

WHAT KEEPS MY BONES TOGETHER?

Ligaments. When two bones come together at a joint, like your elbow or your knee, they are not directly attached. Tough, stretchy straps called ligaments surround them. They join the joints. If you injure a ligament badly the joint could slip apart.

HOW MANY HAIRS ARE ON A PERSON'S HEAD?

I THINK I NEED A HAIRCUT!

The average is about 125,000 hairs, but they would be very hard to count. Head hair is always falling out and growing in. About 50 to 75 hairs fall out each day.

WHAT GIVES MY EYES THEIR COLOR?

The iris. The iris surrounds the pupil, the opening at the center, and controls the amount of light that passes through the hole. The back of the iris has pigment—called melanin—that protects it from light. This is the color we see. If you have blue or green-colored eyes, the iris has small amounts of melanin. Larger amounts of the pigment give you brown or hazel eyes.

WHAT ARE TEARS FOR?

Tears are cleaning fluid for the eye. They come from the lacrimal glands, which sit above the outer edge of each eye. And tears keep coming. Every time you blink, they cover your eye and wash away dirt and germs. When you cry, tears may help you get rid of extra chemicals that build up in your body.

WHAT CAUSES AN ALLERGY?

A mistake. Your body has an army to defend you against germs. The main soldiers are white blood cells, which create antibodies to attack specific germs. But sometimes the white cells act as if harmless foreign substances, like dust or pollen, are dangerous. They cause your nose to run, your eyes to tear, and your skin to itch.

THIS IS NOT MY DAY!

SNIFF- SNIFF!

ONLY THREE?

How many different kinds of rocks are there?

Even though rocks are everywhere, they are all variations of only three basic kinds. *Sedimentary* rocks, like limestone, are formed near the surface of the earth when erosion causes sand, pebbles, and shells to get buried in layers. *Igneous* rocks, like granite, were once liquid lava, which cooled and became hard. *Metamorphic* rocks, like slate, are sedimentary or igneous rocks changed by underground heat and pressure.

What are sponges made of?

Sponges are animals that live on the bottom of the ocean and never move (there is one freshwater variety). Some have beautiful and fantastic colors. Sponges have a skeleton, cells that form chambers, and whip-like threads called *flagella* to capture tiny plants and animals for food.

How long does it take food to pass through my body?

About a day. Eat a burger today and it's gone tomorrow. Digestion—the breaking up of food into chemicals the body can use—begins with the saliva in the mouth, continues in the stomach, the small intestines, and then the large intestines. Your intestines, one long tube all coiled up, can be up to 30 feet long! They absorb nutrients and water from food, as it moves on down the line.

WHY CAN'T I BLOW BUBBLES WITH REGULAR GUM?

Trees have the secret ingredient. All gum contains gum base, sweeteners, and wood resin. Bubble gum has more wood resin, which provides the glue and the stretch. Without as much resin, regular gum isn't elastic enough to expand and hold the bubble you blow.

WHO WAS ALBERT EINSTEIN?

A Nobel Prize-winning physicist, and one of the greatest scientists (1879–1955) of the 20th century. He is famous for his 1905 theory of relativity, which says that time would pass more slowly if you could travel very, very fast. He is also famous for figuring out that mass (matter) and energy are equivalent—that is, they are one and the same, only in different forms. Written as an equation, $E=mc^2$, this discovery led to the development of nuclear power. He also explained the existence of black holes in space and the source of the sun's energy. Einstein was born and grew up in Germany where, amazingly, he was a terrible student as a boy!

When was the first car invented?

In 1770, Nicolas Cugnot, a French soldier, built a steam engine that travelled about three miles per hour. It was so big that this "self-propelled road vehicle" was impossible to steer. In 1862, J. J. Etienne Lenoir, of Paris, took his carriage with an internal combustion engine for its first ride: six miles in three hours at an average speed of two miles per hour.

HOW BIG WAS THE BIGGEST ICEBERG EVER?

Bigger than some countries! In 1956, an iceberg was sighted that was 208 miles long and 60 miles wide. That's about the size of Belgium. Only a small part of this ice monster was seen above water. Most icebergs hide nine-tenths of their size under the surface.

THAT'S A LOT OF ICE!

What causes twins?

"Identical" twins are born when one fertilized egg splits into two. They are the same sex and look alike. "Fraternal" twins are born when two eggs are fertilized. They can be a boy and a girl, or both the same sex. They usually resemble each other no more than any other siblings.

YOU LOOK LIKE ME!

YOU LOOK LIKE ME!

Why do plants turn to face the light?

Not to get a tan. Their leaves, which contain chlorophyll, *create food in combination with light. So they must face the sun. They also have growth substances, which gather in the stem cells that do not face the light. This creates more growth on the shaded side than on the sunny side, which causes the plant to bend toward the light.*

What are the Great Sphinx and the pyramids?

HAVE YOU SEEN A MUMMY?

Along with the Egyptian pyramids, the Great Sphinx is one of the oldest stone structures in the world. The 4,500-year-old sphinx represents the god Horus, who guarded temples and tombs. It has the body of a lion and the face of the pharaoh, or king, who built it to guard his pyramid. Slaves and ancient Egyptians built the pyramids as tombs for their pharaohs. It took tens of thousands of men over 20 years to erect the largest, the 480-foot Great Pyramid built around 2600 B.C. There are still over 80 pyramids in Egypt today.

HOW DOES A SPIDER SPIN A WEB?

Spiders manufacture silk in their bodies—but not the kind of silk we wear. At the end of their abdomens, they have *spinnerets*, which produce silk threads for web building. The silk is elastic and sticky. The spider fastens a thread to an anchoring point like a leaf or twig and draws out more line. As the web grows the spider can walk on it like a tightrope and attach lines in any design.

I LIKE THIS DESIGN!

Where was the world's largest birthday party?

In Buffalo, New York, on July 4, 1991, about 75,000 people sang "Happy Birthday" during a Friendship Festival that's held every year. Buffalo, not far from Canada, was celebrating the birthdays of both countries.

I HAVE SEEDS!

I DON'T!

I WASN'T INVITED TO THAT BIRTHDAY PARTY!

What's the difference between fruits and vegetables?

Seeds make the difference. Any fleshy part of a plant that grows from a flower is called its "fruit." If this part contains seeds, like an orange, an apple, a peach, or even a tomato, it's considered a fruit. If it has no seeds, like broccoli or lettuce or carrots, it's considered a vegetable.

Who was Queen Elizabeth I?

Queen Elizabeth I was England's queen from 1558 to 1603. She brought peace and prosperity to her devoted subjects, who called her "Good Queen Bess." She never married or shared her reign, and during her era—the Elizabethan Age—literature, drama, and music flourished. What a grand time it was!

Why is the sea salty?

There's salt in there. The salt content of an ocean is 3.5% by weight. The salt originates in rocks on the edges of the sea and in rivers and streams. Through the constant wetting and drying, the salt dissolves into the water and collects in the oceans.

I WASN'T INVITED TO THAT BIRTHDAY PARTY EITHER!

HOW DID PEOPLE CLEAN THEIR TEETH BEFORE TOOTHBRUSHES?

The natural way—twigs. People picked a good-tasting twig, chewed one end until it shredded, and used the "bristles." Or, they dipped their fingers in salt and rubbed their teeth. Three hundred years ago wooden-handled, hog-bristled toothbrushes were invented. In some places, they are still used.

... AND I DON'T NEED BATTERIES!

What makes a firefly light up?

Other fireflies! Fireflies (also called lightning bugs) blink their lights in a code that tells what species they are, whether they are male or female, and whether they are ready to mate. The light, produced by a chemical reaction in a special organ in the firefly's abdomen, may also serve as a warning.

... AND I SEE MY DENTIST TWICE A YEAR!

WHO WERE THE AZTECS?

A wandering people who called themselves the Mexica, and lived in what is now central Mexico from around 1150 to 1550. An Aztec god told their leader they should stop wandering when they saw an eagle perched on a cactus eating a snake. The Aztecs found this eagle on a small island in a lake. Because they had no farmland, they invented a way to make floating islands on the lake on which they could live and grow food. Today, the center of this area is Mexico City, the capital of Mexico. The Aztecs are famed for their art, poetry, science and for having created a solar calendar lasting 365 days. One of the creepy things about the Aztecs is that, at temples built on top of pyramids, they sacrificed people to their gods at least 18 times a year!

> I CAN RUN FASTER THAN YOU!

> SURE YOU CAN.

> I'M NOT CLIMBING UP TO THAT TEMPLE ANY TIME SOON!

WHAT'S THE DIFFERENCE BETWEEN A CAMEL AND A DROMEDARY?

One hump or two. There are two types of camels. Bactrian camels have two humps. The dromedary is a one-humped Arabian camel especially bred for riding and racing. These long-legged beasts can run about 10 miles an hour and travel as far as 100 miles a day.

WHAT IS THE OLDEST TREE IN THE WORLD?

The currently living oldest tree is a 4,600-year-old bristle-cone pine in California's White Mountains. The *inside* of a tree, not the outside, reveals its age. The number of rings seen on a tree stump or cut log tells the tree's age. Each ring is about a year's growth of wood cells.

THAT'S NOT A MEMBER OF MY FAMILY!

AT LEAST I DON'T HAVE DANDRUFF!

HOW DOES A SUBMARINE WORK?

Ballast is the key. It controls the weight of a ship. A submarine uses seawater kept in ballast tanks. The tanks are filled with water to make the ship heavier when it dives. To make the submarine lighter when it wants to surface, the water is forced out of the tanks by compressed air. Mechanical fins called hydroplanes direct the boat upward and downward.

WHY DO WE HAVE HAIR?

It used to be our coat. Prehistoric humans had hair all over their body to keep warm. Today, our eyebrows, eyelashes, and the hair in our nose and ears helps keep out dust. But what about the rest? We still have fine hair over most parts of our body—5 million hairs is the average for both men and women. But scientists don't know exactly why.

WHAT MAKES SNOW?

First the temperature has to be below freezing. Then a drop of water vapor may form a crystal around a particle of dust in the atmosphere. Some crystals stick together and form snowflakes heavy enough to fall to Earth. All snowflakes are different. The individual crystals are the same, but no two combinations are identical.

How many species of bats are there?

So many that it's hard to keep count. About 900 to 1,000 different species have been identified. Bats live in almost every part of the globe, except in very cold places, such as the Arctic, sub-Arctic, and Antarctic. How many individual bats are there? That is impossible to say, but some experts estimate that there are hundreds of millions of bats per species!

THAT'S A LOT OF WATERING!

HOW MANY DIFFERENT PLANTS ARE THERE IN THE WORLD?

More than we know. About 350,000 species of plants are known, but new ones are constantly being discovered. Plants range from algae to orchids to giant sequoia trees, and they're a hardy bunch. They've been on the planet for 3 billion years. Animal life didn't join them until about 600 million years ago.

WHAT'S THE DIFFERENCE BETWEEN A WHITE EGG AND A BROWN EGG?

It's in the chicken. Some breeds of chickens lay white eggs and some brown. The eggs fry, scramble, boil, and taste the same.

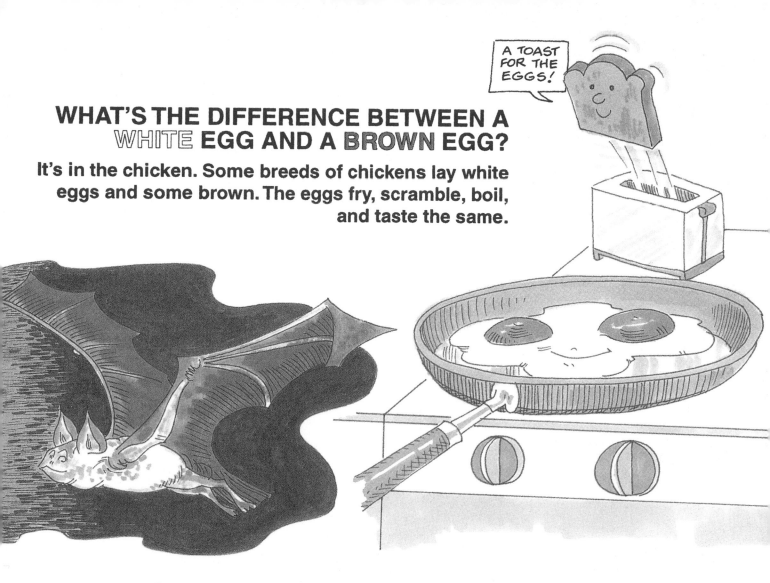

A TOAST FOR THE EGGS!

WHY CAN'T I TASTE ANYTHING WHEN I HAVE A COLD?

Because your nose is stuffed. Both your nose and your tongue have special cells that send messages to the brain about smells and tastes. In tasting, they work together. So, when you have a cold and your nose is lined with mucus, your smell cells are not getting the news that your tongue is tasting an orange. It's the pits.

WHO WERE THE INCAS?

Ancient people of the Andes Mountains who lived in an area that included parts of what are now Peru, Chile, and Ecuador. From the 1200s to 1500s their civilization grew to become the largest in the New World. The Incas are known for their pottery and cloth, and for their extraordinary engineering. In high mountains they constructed terraced farms, aqueducts, miles of stone roads (with bridges and tunnels!), and a city in the clouds, Machu Picchu—all of which still remain. Machu Picchu sits on a mountain ridge over a mile and a half above sea level!

How many ants are in an ant colony?

I'M AN ANT AND AN UNCLE!

That depends on the type of ant—and there are about 15,000 different kinds! But most ants are *social* insects that live in groups. Some colonies have only 10 ants and others have hundreds of thousands. Some nests are "hills," others are underground, and still others are built from leaves or found in wood. Wherever they live, ants will usually come out if you have a picnic.

WHY DO PEOPLE HAVE DIFFERENT COLOR SKINS?

The difference is only skin deep. Melanin is the substance in the skin that produces darker shades. Since melanin protects the skin from the sun, more cells are created when we are exposed to the sun, and the skin becomes darker. The theory is that, in ancient times, people who lived in sunny climates were darker skinned, and those that lived in colder areas were fair. People today have inherited the color of their ancestors.

WHAT WOULD HAPPEN IF ALL THE *ICE* IN THE WORLD MELTED?

I HAD BETTER LEARN TO SWIM!

Some people would have to move. The seas would rise about 200 feet and the coasts of continents would gradually disappear under water. Floods in America would claim major centers like New York and San Fransisco. But don't panic. Although the earth's ice has begun to melt at a surprising rate, scientists who study this phenomenon say it will take thousands of years for seas to rise this much.

WHY DO MAGNETS ATTRACT?

Iron contains millions of tiny magnets called domains. Usually they are pointed in different directions and are not magnetized. A magnetized metal has all of its domains pointing in the same direction. All magnets have two poles, north and south, that pull iron and steel objects toward them, into their *magnetic field.* They only attract their opposites, north to south and south to north.

Why does hot water clean better than cold water?

It heats things up. Whatever's stuck on you dissolves better in heat. Soap grabs grease better in heat. And bacteria (tiny organisms that may carry disease) die in heat. Heat cleans things up.

I WAS WONDERING ABOUT THAT MYSELF!

HOW DO SNAKES MOVE IF THEY DON'T HAVE LEGS?

With a combination of muscles, scales, and an amazingly flexible spine. Snakes have belly scales, which grip the ground like tractor treads while their muscles pull their bodies forward. The spine is responsible for the snake's trademark curvy slither.

HOW IS PAPER MADE?

THIS IS GENUINE 100% PAPER!

It all starts with wood. Cut, ground up, mashed, watered, bleached, pressed, rolled out, and dried, wood becomes paper. Logs are ground up and combined with water and chemicals into a mixture called pulp. Shredded rags, glue, and coloring are added to make some papers. Then the pulp is dried and pressed into giant rolls.

What's my funny bone?

It's not humorous . . . it's *humerus.* That's your funny-bone's real name. It connects with the bones of your fore-arm at the elbow, a place where there are a bunch of sensitive nerves. When you whack that spot, it's no joke.

WHAT'S SO FUNNY?

WHO WAS THE FIRST PERSON IN SPACE?

When Russian Cosmonaut Yuri Alekseyevich Gagarin took off on April 12, 1961, he was the first person to leave the Earth in a satellite. He was up there alone for 108 minutes. Before returning, he traveled 17,560 miles. Although unafraid, Yuri must have been in a hurry.

HI!

?

WHY DO I FEEL DIZZY WHEN I SPIN AROUND?

You're making waves in your ears. Inside your ears are three semicircular canals filled with liquid. The ends of these tubes have nerves in a jelly-like substance that tell your brain your head's position. When your head spins, the liquid rocks and the jelly rolls. If you stop suddenly, everything keeps moving for a moment. *That's* when you feel dizzy.

SHE'S MAKING ME DIZZY JUST WATCHING HER !!!

COME ON DOWN!

WHAT ANIMAL GATHERS IN THE LARGEST GROUP?

The seal. Each year about 1.5 million Alaskan fur seals gather on the Pribilof Islands off the coast of Alaska to breed. The result: 500,000 baby seals.

HOW DOES A PARACHUTE WORK?

Perfectly . . . or else! When brave men and women jump out of airplanes, they pull a cord, and a canopy, or parachute, opens above them. This umbrella-shaped cloth resists the air, counteracts the jumper's weight, and slows the fall. When the person hits the ground, the force is about the same as a long jump.

HOW MUCH WATER IS THERE IN A WATERMELON?

Ninety-three percent! That means a 10-pound watermelon has 9.3 pounds of water. Is it a fruit or a drink? A fruit drink!

WHAT'S THE DIFFERENCE BETWEEN A COMET AND A SHOOTING STAR?

Shooting stars are meteors that burn up in the Earth's atmosphere. Comets consist of mostly frozen gas, ice, and dust. Unlike planets, neither circles the sun, but they do orbit in space. Comets have fiery tails, which we see when they pass the Earth. The heat of the sun turns the ice into gas, which forms the comet's tail as it escapes.

What is the Great Wall of China?

One of the largest and most ambitious building projects ever undertaken. Over several centuries, beginning in the 7th century B.C., the people of ancient China built the wall to keep out invaders.

The most important work was led by Shih Huangdi, who became emperor in 221 B.C. He united China's many warring territories into one nation. To defend it, he had the wall's many parts joined into one continous defensive line. Not counting branches and side sections, it is nearly 4,160 miles long!

WHAT'S THE HOTTEST PLACE IN THE UNITED STATES?

The hottest temperature ever recorded in the United States was 134°F in Death Valley, California, on July 10, 1913. It was not a cool summer. The thermometer hit 120°F for 43 days in a row.

THIS IS HOT!

WHAT CAUSES A TORNADO?

A tornado forms in storm clouds when masses of hot, humid air rise and begin to rotate. The rotating funnel cloud can extend down to the ground and destroy everything in its path. (The quicker the spin—some rotate faster than 300 miles an hour—the more powerful the tornado.) A tornado's funnel, which can be from 50 feet to a mile wide, travels with a storm cloud at an average speed of 30 to 40 miles an hour.

WHEN WAS THE CHOCOLATE BAR INVENTED?

In 1811. A chocolate drink was first brought to Europe from the Aztecs of Mexico in the 1500s. Three hundred years later, Francois-Louis Cailler of Switzerland manufactured the first chocolate in bars. How many things can you think of that have chocolate in them?

HOW DOES A PLANE STAY UP IN THE AIR?

SO, THAT'S HOW I FLY!

I DON'T HAVE WINGS!

Power and lift. Power comes from the engines. Lift comes from the wings, which are called airfoils. Airfoils are rounded on top, flat on the bottom, rounded on the front edge, and narrow at the back. Because of this shape, there is less air pressure on the top of the wing. The greater pressure under the wing pushes upward and keeps the plane from falling.

OUCH!

Who Was King Arthur?

Arthur, an English king, is believed to have lived in the 6th century. No one is absolutely sure, but the legends about him are fantastic. They say that he was the only man to withdraw a magical sword from a stone. His Knights of the Round Table included Sir Lancelot and Sir Galahad, the greatest soldiers in Europe. And Arthur was supposedly handsome, courageous, and honest. It would be nice to know he really existed.

What's the star nearest to Earth?

Don't wait for dark to find it. Don't even take out your telescope. It's our very own daytime star, the sun, just 93 million miles away. The next closest star is Proxima Centauri, and it's 25 trillion miles from Earth.

WHAT IS ACID RAIN?

It's worse than bad weather. It's rain carrying chemical pollution. When industries burn coal and oil, sulfur and nitrogen rise into the air and dissolve in the atmosphere. When moisture forms, these chemicals become part of the water vapor that falls to the earth as rain.

COUGH! COUGH!

WHAT WAS THE WORLD'S FIRST DOG?

I KNEW HIM WELL!

A wolf-like creature. The wolf is a member of the scientific family Canidae, which developed about 20 million years ago. All dogs are related to this same ancestor and are part of the same family. But today, there are many different dogs because of *selective breeding*. People have bred dogs with certain characteristics until a whole line of descendants developed. Now the world has big dogs and small, long and short-haired, pointy and floppy-eared, making the tiny Chihuahua and huge St. Bernard strange, but true relatives.

I FLEW BEFORE THEM!

WHO INVENTED THE FIRST POWERED AIRCRAFT?

The Wright brothers, Orville and Wilbur. When their biplane (a plane with two sets of wings) rose above the ground at Kitty Hawk, North Carolina, in 1903, it was the first flight powered by an engine. First it bumped along, but on the fourth try, Wilbur was airborne for 59 seconds and flew 852 feet.

WHO WAS THE ORIGINAL DRACULA?

The main character in an 1897 novel by Englishman Bram Stoker. The author based his story "on a king Vlad Dracula," who lived in the 1400s in Wallachia, a part of Romania. He was better known as Vlad the Impaler for his nasty habit of sticking the bodies of his enemies on wooden stakes like a fence. He is said to have once impaled 20,000 people as a warning to the invading Turks.

I CAN'T STAY... I'M LATE FOR LUNCH!

FEET DO YOUR THING!!

I'D RATHER SEE THE MOVIE!!

HOW DO EARTHWORMS HELP THE GROUND?

They make the ground good for plants. Creeping and crawling, earthworms loosen up the soil so plants can wiggle their roots down. Also, by leaving waste behind, earthworms fertilize the ground for growing plants.

WHAT MAKES ICE CUBES CRACK WHEN YOU PUT THEM IN A DRINK?

I HEARD THAT!

A temperature clash. When the ice cube meets the liquid, its outside begins to warm up and expand. But its icy center remains frozen and unmoved. Pressure between the outer, expanding part of the cube and its frozen center builds up until...*snap!*—the ice cube cracks.

What kinds of instruments are in a symphony orchestra?

LET'S BEGIN.

A ONE AND A TWO AND A THREE!

WAIT FOR ME!

I'M READY!

The sound of a symphony is a mix of different families of instruments: *percussion*, like the drums and cymbals; *brass*, like the trumpet and trombone; *woodwinds*, like the flute and clarinet; and *strings*, like the violin and cello. Ninety to 120 players put it all together—and the result is sweet music.

LET'S EAT!

WHY DO MY CHEEKS GET RED IN THE WINTER?

It's warm blood coming to the rescue of your cold skin. In winter, you wear a hat, coat, and gloves but probably not a face mask. So your body, all on its own, sends more rosy, warm blood to the vessels under your cheeks. It protects your face from frostbite.

WHO ATE THE FIRST SANDWICH?

Someone who was too busy to use silverware. The honor goes to an Englishman named, of course, the Earl of Sandwich. In the 1700s, he put some food between two slices of bread, took a bite, and made history.

What do red giants, white dwarves, and black holes have in common?

Stardom. But not the Hollywood type. Having burned off most of their helium and hydrogen fuel, they are all stars nearing the end of their existence. The dying star first swells and becomes a red giant. Then its enormous gravitational force shrinks it down into a white dwarf, still giving off some light. But a black hole does not. If the star is massive enough, its gravitational pull is so strong that even light can't escape its surface.

WHY DO POLICE USE FINGERPRINTS AND DNA TO TRACE PEOPLE?

Because the information in your cells is yours alone. In the case of fingerprints, the loops, whorls, and arches that form the line patterns on your fingers are unique to you. No two people have the same pattern—not even identical twins. The reason police use DNA to trace people is that sometimes fingerprints can't be found. If hair or skin cells are available, however, the DNA, or unique structural information within human cells, can be identified and traced. Like fingerprints, no two people have the same DNA—*except* for identical twins!

UP, UP, AND AWAY!

Hot-Air Balloons

Want a quiet ride? Try a balloon. Hot-air balloons float when the air inside the balloon is heated. The heated air is lighter than the cool air outside, so the balloon rises toward the sky. Once released, the balloon will float as high as its weight allows. Then the pilot must throw weight off to go higher, or release air to descend.

HAVE A NICE FLIGHT!

HELICOPTERS

Want to hang out? Take a helicopter ride. Helicopters can hover, or hang in the air, over one spot. The *rotor blades* above the cockpit are the "wings" that provide the lift and the direction. At a certain speed, the blades hold the helicopter in one spot. At a faster speed, the blades will lift it higher. Tilted, they send the aircraft backward, forward, and sideways. A small rotor on the tail completes the balancing act.

JET PLANE

Want to travel fast? Take a jet plane. The jet engine is called a turbofan. Fans at the front of the engine suck air into a compression chamber, where it is mixed with fuel and fired. The heated, high-pressure air and the exhaust gases rush out the back of the engine and thrust the plane forward. The first jet plane took off in 1947.

Blimp

Want to travel light? Fly by blimp. A blimp is a cabin carried by a huge balloon filled with helium, a gas seven times lighter than air. The rising or upthrust of this balloon is so powerful that it can carry an engine, along with cabin and passengers. Small propellers and rudder do the steering. Early blimps, or airships as they were called, carried as many as 200 people, but today only the smaller variety—the blimp—is still in use.

ROCKET

Want to blast off? Ride a rocket. A rocket is a heat engine with solid or liquid fuel, called a *propellant*. The basic principle of a rocket is the same as a firecracker. A highly flammable substance is packed into a chamber and fired. The hot gases that result stream out from the base and drive the rocket upward. It takes five huge rockets to shoot a space shuttle into orbit.

Who was Leonardo da Vinci?

THAT'S ME!

A genius. Leonardo (1452–1519) lived during the Italian Renaissance, a great artistic period. He is famous as a painter, and his work, the *Mona Lisa* is one of the most valuable paintings in the world. But he was also a scientist, inventor, engineer, architect, and designer. He made brilliant observations that paved the way for future scientists and inventors.

WHAT'S FOR LUNCH?

HOW DO PLANTS EAT?

They make food. They cook up sugars using the process of *photosynthesis*, which combines sunlight, carbon dioxide, and water from the soil. *Chlorophyll*, a green pigment which captures the sun's energy, makes this possible. Some plants that can't get what they need from the soil dine on insects. They capture them with sticky leaves—or petals that snap together like jaws.

I'M THE DRUMMER BOY.

WHY DO SOLDIERS SALUTE?

It's a military rule. A salute is a sign of respect to a person of higher rank. Bowing or kneeling to royalty or officers has gone on throughout history. A hand-to-the-forehead salute probably comes from taking off a hat as a gesture of respect—which may have come from the way knights removed their helmets when speaking to nobles.

I-I-I'M C-C-COLD!

WHAT IS THE LARGEST ORGAN IN MY BODY?

THE LAYER THAT PROTECTS ALL OF YOU—YOUR SKIN. AN ADULT MAN HAS ABOUT 20 SQUARE FEET OF SKIN, A WOMAN, 17 SQUARE FEET. (THAT'S IF IT WERE TAKEN OFF AND LAID OUT TO MEASURE.) SKIN FLAKES OFF ALL THE TIME. IT TAKES ABOUT A MONTH FOR NEW TISSUE TO REPLACE OLD.

When was the first zipper zipped?

In 1893, but it didn't stay closed for long. This first version, for boots and shoes, didn't work well. In 1913, Gideon Sundback invented a zipper that stayed zipped. Nobody cared until World War I in 1917, when zippers began appearing on military uniforms. Still, it wasn't until 1938 that the zipper replaced the buttons on men's pants.

IS THE EARTH GETTING WARMER?

Yes. The earth has gone from warmer to colder and back again over the course of millions of years. But for the past 100 years the average temperature has been steadily rising, with a more rapid increase in the last 20 years.

In 2007, a report issued by 800 climate researchers that was approved by 2,500 scientists from 130 countries concluded that the earth was indeed getting warmer and that human activity is partly responsible.

Who invented the ice-cream cone?

Italo Marcioni. He got a patent for a special cone mold in 1903. But ice cream didn't really meet cone in a big way until 1904 at the St. Louis Fair. An ice-cream vendor was next to a waffle maker. One rolled up a waffle—the other put ice cream in it. The rest is history.

What makes whirlpools whirl?

Water that flows in a certain direction is called a current. When two currents collide, the force forms a swirl of water. Currents whipped by the wind, pulled by the tides, and interrupted by rocks can also form whirlpools. Some are powerful enough to suck down whatever gets caught in the middle.

GULP!

HOW DO THE HOLES GET INTO SWISS CHEESE?

Bacteria puts them there. Cheese is a food whose flavor and texture is created by bacteria. The holes in Swiss cheese are made by "bubbles" of gas given off by its busy builders.

WHAT IS THE WORLD'S MOST POPULOUS CITY?

Tokyo, Japan. In 2005, Tokyo's metropolitan area – the city and its adjacent areas – had a population of 35 million people.

HOW DOES A LIGHTBULB LIGHT UP?

With a de*light*ful combination of electricity, metal, heat, and gas. Inside a bulb is a thin filament (wire) of tungsten, a metal with a very high melting point. That means it can take a lot of heat without melting. Electrical current heats the filament (as high as 4,500 degrees!) so that it glows with light. The bulb is airtight and filled with an inactive gas called argon, which keeps oxygen out and helps the bulb last longer.

WHAT ARE ROBOTS USED FOR?

Robots are good at doing the same task over and over again, exactly the same way. All robots are machines that have computer instructions built in. They paint cars. They lift heavy loads. They enter radioactive or hot areas too dangerous for humans. Some are simply arms and a gripper, with humans controlling them from a distance.

WHAT IS

MIRROR

GAS FILLED TUBE

ELECTRODE

ELECTRODE

SEMI-SILVERED MIRROR

How does a compact disc player work?

It uses laser light and a computer to change codes into sounds. Under its surface, a disc has tiny parts arranged in patterns in circular tracks. These patterns are computer coded and there are 600 million on a disc! As the disc spins, a laser light reads the patterns, sending electrical signals to a computer. The player's computer has a memory of all the possible signals, and turns the code into sounds.

WHAT ARE X RAYS?

Rays of energy similar to light rays. But unlike light, they travel *through* you. When an X ray is taken, the rays penetrate your body and strike a piece of photographic film. The result is a shadow picture of your insides. Denser parts, like bones, are brighter because they absorb X rays. Fleshy parts are dimmer because the rays pass through them.

A LASER?

A very intense bean of light. Lasers are created when the molecules of gases, liquids, or solids are so excited by electricity that they burst into a single, concentrated, powerful stream of light. Some cut through steel or drill holes in diamonds. Others perform everyday tasks. Lasers are used to play audio discs and read the bar codes on groceries.

IS THERE LIFE ON OTHER PLANETS?

TAKE ME TO YOUR LEADER.

For sure, there are no little green creatures with melon heads and almond-shaped eyes in our solar system. But frozen or even liquid water may exist beneath the red Martian soil, as well as on several moons that revolve around some of our other planets. Europa, a moon of Jupiter, may have deep oceans of water beneath its icy surface. And where there is water, there could be living organisms.

Beyond our solar system there are other planets revolving around some of the billions and billions of stars in outer space, and a few of them may be similar to Earth.

WHO CREATED THE ALPHABET?

For thousands of years people drew pictures, creating a symbol—like a drawing of the sun—to stand for an object or an idea. The ancient Egyptians and other Middle Eastern peoples were the first to communicate this way. That was about 5,000 years ago. About 3,000 years ago, the Greeks had a complete alphabet. The Greek alphabet was further changed by the Romans in the first century A.D. It's the Roman alphabet that English is based on. You can see the history in the word "alphabet." It comes from the first two letters of the Greek alphabet, alpha and beta.

Do all birds sing?

No. Most birds make some kind of sound, but bird-song is different from calls, squawks, chattering, or caws. Among the various species known as songbirds, males are usually the only ones that sing. They do it to let females know that they are available for mating. Sometimes, they sing to let other males know that they are claiming a certain territory.

WHERE WERE THE FIRST OLYMPICS HELD?

Olympia, Greece. The ancient Greek Olympics, held over 2,000 years ago, are the inspiration for today's games. The Greeks ended their games in 393 B.C., and it wasn't until 1896 that the games began again as an international event. The world has missed only three Olympics: in 1916, 1940, and 1944, because of the two world wars.

TO OLYMPICS

WANT TO RACE?

WHY ARE SO MANY PEOPLE RIGHT-HANDED?

Your brain decides. But there are still some things about the brain that scientists don't know—and this is one of them. Nine out of ten people are right-handed. Nobody knows why.

How can I get SUNBURNED on a cloudy day?

If it's daytime, the sun is out whether we can see it or not. The sun's energy reaches us mostly as heat and light, but 6% of the light is ultraviolet radiation (UVR), which causes sunburn. Clouds and pollution block some UVR, but the sun's rays are so strong that dangerous amounts still reach us.

How do crickets make their sound?

They wing it. Crickets, like most insects, have no vocal chords. But they do have some things to say, like "Hello," or "Here I am." Crickets make a noise by rubbing the hard, ridged tips of their wings together. That's cricket communication, but it's music to *our* ears.

I DON'T PLAY CRICKET.

Why do the continents look as though they fit together like a jigsaw puzzle?

One theory is that the Earth was once a huge single land mass that broke up. Over millions of years, pieces slowly drifted apart and became the continents as we know them today. The continents and the oceans have gigantic plates beneath them that move very slowly. So the positions of the continents are always changing ever so slightly.

IT FITS!

Who invented ROCK 'N' ROLL?

It was born in the 1950s. It grew from rhythm and blues music played by African-American artists like Chuck Berry, Little Richard, and others. Combined with gospel, folk, and country and western music, it came together in a new sound. Elvis Presley sold millions of rock 'n' roll records and became known as the "King of Rock 'n' Roll." When the Beatles brought their music from England in the 1960s, rock 'n' roll was here to stay.

I DIDN'T KNOW THAT!

WHAT IS A MUMMY?

It's not necessarily what most people think of—an Egyptian corpse wrapped in cloth. When bacteria and fungi cannot grow in a dead body, it becomes *mummified*. A mummy still has some of the body's soft tissues (skin, muscles, or organs). Some mummies were made by *embalming*, which is any process used to preserve a dead body. Ancient Egyptians did this with linen and tree resin (sap) because they believed in preparing the body for life after death. However, humans and animals have been found naturally mummified all over the world, usually in very dry or very cold places.

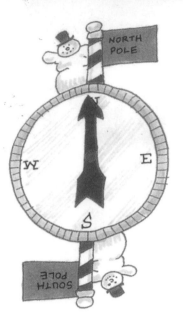

Why does a compass always point North?

There's an invisible, but not mysterious, force at work. The needle on a compass is a thin, freely swinging magnet. The earth is also a magnet—a giant one, with magnetic ends at each of its poles. No one is sure why it is like this, but scientists think that electric currents in a liquid core inside the earth might be the cause. The North Pole, which has a strong magnetic force, attracts the needle on a compass, causing it to point north.

WHY DOES SOME SPOILED FOOD TURN GREEN?

It's the dreaded mold. Mold is all around us in the air and in the ground. It's a kind of fungus that grows in moist places, on food left out on the counter, and even on forgotten food in the back of the refrigerator. The tiny bits of mold grow into a large, green colony.

HOW OLD IS THE EARTH?

Very old—about 4.6 billion years. Primitive forms of life, like algae and bacteria, began to appear about a billion years later, when the planet developed the water and oxygen necessary to support living things. Fossils exist that show primitive life forms from 3.5 billion years ago.

WHY DO I GET A SCAB WHEN I GET A CUT?

WHY DO PEOPLE DRESS IN COSTUMES ON HALLOWEEN?

To scare away the ghosts. In ancient times, the Celtic peoples of the British Isles prepared themselves for the dark days of winter with a festival. They lit bonfires and sacrificed animals. They expected evil spirits to be roaming about. To hide from them, they dressed up in costumes.

Who was Hans Christian Andersen?

A Danish storyteller who lived during the 1800s. He is known as "the father of the modern fairy tale," and wrote such well known tales as "The Ugly Duckling," "The Emperor's New Clothes," "The Princess and the Pea," and 165 others. Hans Christian Andersen was the son of a shoemaker and a washerwoman. His mother couldn't even read. But his parents encouraged in Hans a love of folktales and literature, which led to his becoming a beloved, world-famous author of fairy tales.

It's a natural bandage. Healthy blood cells come to the rescue of skin cells torn by a cut. They thicken and clot, and add chemicals and other substances, which dry, shrink, and harden the cut cells. Then they become a scab—a seal that keeps blood in and germs out.

Why are some clouds white ...while others are gray or... black?

Because clouds are masses of water droplets and ice crystals. Sometimes shadows make clouds look gray. But usually, the more dense the water within a cloud, the grayer it is—and the sooner the rain.

IT'S NOT RAINING!

IT'S RAINING!

CAN ALL BIRDS FLY?

WHY SHOULD I FLY? I'M NOT GOING ANYWHERE!

Not big birds. Not the penguin, nor the ostrich. The shape of giant birds like the ostrich, the South American rhea, and the Australian emu keeps them from flying, as much as their weight does. Small birds have enormous breast muscles relative to the rest of their streamlined bodies that enable them to flap their wings and fly. Big birds don't.

WHERE IS THE WORLD'S LONGEST CAVE?

The Mammoth Cave and Flint Ridge cave system in Kentucky have many interconnected cave passages. Together, they form a system with an overall length of 348 miles—and counting!

WHAT IS A TSUNAMI?

A series of giant waves created by a violent shake-up of the ocean's floor, such as an earthquake or a volcanic eruption. Moving at an average speed of 450 miles an hour, these waves gain height and power. A *tsunami* (soo-NAH-mee) may be only three feet high in open sea, but may tower as high as 100 feet by the time it reaches land.

THAT'S *FAST!*

If the Earth is *moving,* why can't we feel it?

I DON'T FEEL A THING!

MAYBE THAT'S WHY I ACT DIZZY!!

Gravity keeps our feet on the ground. Even though Earth is spinning very fast—at about 1,083 miles per hour at the surface—we don't feel it. That is because we are on or close to Earth's surface, moving along at the same speed.

What's the difference between an alligator

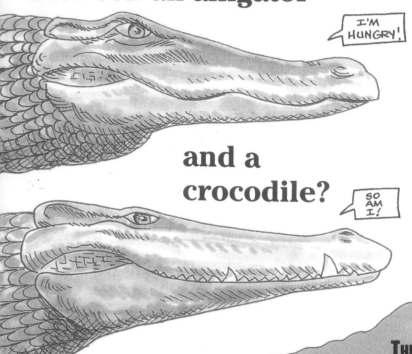

I'M HUNGRY!

and a crocodile?

SO AM I!

An alligator has a broader, rounder snout. A crocodile's snout is thinner and pointier. When a crocodile closes its mouth, the larger teeth on its bottom jaw rest in spaces on the **outside** of its upper jaw. In an alligator's mouth, they rest on the **inside** of the jaw.

HOW DO MOLES LIVE UNDERGROUND?

FOR RENT

THEY CONSTANTLY DIG TUNNELS WITH THEIR STRONG FRONT CLAWS SEARCHING FOR TASTY WORMS AND GRUBS TO EAT. THE TUNNELS ALSO CONNECT THEM TO UNDERGROUND NESTS AND RESTING PLACES. THEIR MOLEHILLS, THE EXCESS EARTH FROM ALL THAT DIGGING, HAVE RUINED MANY A LAWN.

How and why do chameleons change color?

It's hide-and-seek in the animal world every day. Some animals hide while others seek to eat them. The chameleon has a natural ability to hide by changing its colors to match its surroundings. If it stays long enough in one spot, its color cells will change to blend in with the background. They also change color when it's too hot or cold, or if they feel threatened.

I SEE YOU!!

Which waterfall has the most water?

Khone Falls, in Laos, a country in Asia. Its flow of 2.5 million gallons of water per second gives it the greatest volume of any waterfall in the world. That is nearly twice the volume of Niagara Falls, which has the greatest volume of any U.S. waterfall.

Why can I see myself in a mirror?

Everything you see comes from light rays that bounce off objects and bounce back to your eyes. A mirror is glass with a shiny chemical coating on the back. When you stand in front of a mirror, light rays bounce off your body onto the mirror's coating. Then the rays reflect, or bounce back, to your eyes. What you are is what you see—it's your reflection.

WHAT ARE SUNSPOTS?

They're cool. Sunspots are places on the surface of the sun caused by changes in the sun's magnetic field. The surface temperature of the sun is about 10,000°Fahrenheit. Sunspots are about 3,600 degrees cooler. But cool on the sun is still hot, hot, hot.

ARE PEOPLE REALLY WEIGHTLESS IN OUTER SPACE?

Yes, as long as they are in a zero-gravity environment—out of range of the gravity of a planet, moon, or other large body.

People who spend any length of time in space—on a space station, for example—suffer from the effects of weightlessness: They lose body weight as well as calcium from their bones. They usually get back to normal soon after returning to Earth.

WHERE IS THE LARGEST LIBRARY?

The United States Library of Congress in Washington, DC. Know what you want before you go there, because it contains over 134 million items. And don't get lost in the shelves—there are 575 miles of them. The first modern public library in the United States was in New Hampshire in 1833, and it had 700 books. The largest public library today is in Chicago, and it's stacked with 11.4 million books.

WHAT MAKES A VOLCANO *ERUPT?*

A volcano erupting is a...**BLAST!** that comes from below. Volcanoes are located in places where plates are shifting beneath the Earth's crust. In such spots, hot liquid rock (magma) and gases are trying to escape. Pressure from these elements builds up until . . . **WHOOSH!** . . . they shoot up the center of a volcano. Fire, smoke, and ashes leap into the sky and lava pours down the sides of the volcano.

I'M BLOWING MY TOP!

I'D HAVE MY OWN TV SERIES ....IF TV HAD BEEN INVENTED!

WHEN WAS THE FIRST PLAY PERFORMED?

A *long* time ago—around 500 B.C. The first dramatists were the Greeks. They wrote and performed tragedies—serious plays— as well as comedies to make people laugh. Some plays have survived and are still performed today! The ancient Greek plays are considered to be among the great literature of the world.

FUNNY!

SAD!

79

How does the ice in a skating rink keep from MELTING?

Watch your toes, the floor is freezing. Beneath the ice is a concrete floor with pipes that are filled with a freezing solution. An Olympic rink may have up to 11 miles of these chilling pipes. So the weather above doesn't affect the ice as much as the temperature below.

WHO WAS KING TUT?

Tutankhamen (toot-ang-KAH-men) was his name, and he has been called the "boy king" of Egypt. Tut became king in 1361 B.C. when he was only nine years old. He died when he was about 19. His tomb and its fabulous riches weren't discovered until 1922—3,000 years after he was buried. He was found in a coffin made from 2,500 pounds of gold!

IS THERE GOLD AT A RAINBOW'S END?

No such luck. That good-luck tale comes from Irish folklore, in which anyone who reached a rainbow's end would find a leprechaun's pot o' gold.

Not everyone considers a rainbow good luck. In ancient Greece, the word for rainbow was *iris*, named for the goddess of war and unrest. In one African folktale, a rainbow that touched one's house was a snake that brought bad luck.

HOW DOES AN ELECTRIC EEL MAKE ELECTRICITY?

Body batteries. Electric eels, and other fish like the torpedo ray and some catfish, have thousands of linked natural battery cells in a coat of muscle tissue. A six-foot-long South American electric eel can generate a 500-volt zap of electricity—enough to light up a dozen bulbs.

ARE WE RELATED?

HOW SHOCKING!

WHAT IS CORAL?

A coral *polyp* is a tiny ocean animal with a skeleton on the outside and a soft body inside. When the body dies, the skeleton remains. Some corals live in large colonies. Their skeletons, millions and millions of them, form *reefs*, a giant wall of coral in the sea not far from shore. Corals can be shaped like flowers, fans, fingers, or even giant brains.

WHY DON'T FISH SINK?

Many fish have an organ called a swim bladder that helps keep them afloat. A fish remains balanced by changing the amount of air in its swim bladder, which is something like a balloon. Fish take in oxygen from the water around them as it flows in through their gills.

HOW DOES A COMPUTER THINK?

It doesn't. Computers *operate*. They do amazing things, but not without instructions. A computer has four basic units: memory, input, central processing, and output. The **memory** holds programs that tell the computer how to perform different tasks (play games, process words, add numbers, etc.) The **input** unit (keyboard) provides the information (data) that the program will work on. The **processing** unit uses the data to follow the program and work out results. The **output** unit displays the results—on a screen or through a printer.

I DON'T WRITE LETTERS!

EVERYONE WRITES LETTERS!

WHEN WAS THE FIRST POSTAGE STAMP USED?

In 1840 in Great Britain. Queen Victoria's picture was printed on over 60 million stamps called "Penny Blacks." George Washington and Benjamin Franklin were given the same honor in the United States seven years later. Many people collect stamps. One of the first British Penny Blacks was sold in 1991 for over $2 million.

Most people don't care as long as they can eat it, chew it, drink it, or let it melt in their mouths. The cocoa tree and its bean are the source of chocolate. When the beans are melted down, they become liquid cocoa. **DO NOT** drink it. It's so bitter it puckers up your mouth. Lots of sugar is added before it becomes chocolate.

How can a scientist tell how old a fossil is?

Radioactivity—it goes on and on. Mineralized fossils give off small amounts of nuclear radioactivity. The radioactivity slowly decreases over thousands and thousands of years. So scientists can take a bone, measure the changes in radioactivity, and tell how long ago the plant or animal lived.

Why do leaves turn colors in the fall?

OH, NO! IT'S FALL AGAIN!

THE SKY IS FALLING!

For the tree's survival. Trees must shed their leaves to conserve water during the winter. So a film forms where the leaf joins the tree, cutting off food. That's when the colors change. Chlorophyll, which makes the leaf green, begins to break down. All the other colors—yellow, red, gold, and purple—which were hidden by the green, begin to show.

WHY DOES THE MOON CHANGE SHAPE IN THE SKY?

It doesn't. Only what we see changes. The moon circles the entire earth about once every month. The moon reflects the sun's light. As it travels, we see the whole moon or parts of it, depending on where the earth is in relation to the sun. What we see are the moon's *phases,* from a curved sliver to a full moon and back again.

I'M THE ALARM CLOCK FOR THIS FARM.

Why do roosters crow in the morning?

It's their mating call. Roosters crow to attract females. They crow when the light is dim—early morning and just before dark—so their enemies are less likely to see them.

Who was Sitting Bull?

A fierce Native American leader, who tried to keep settlers from taking the land of his people, the Sioux. In 1876, Sitting Bull led nearly 2,000 warriors in one of the greatest defeats of American troops—the Battle of Little Bighorn.

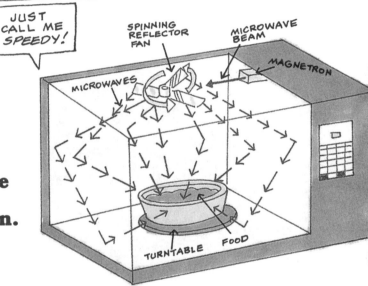

JUST CALL ME SPEEDY!

SPINNING REFLECTOR FAN
MICROWAVE BEAM
MAGNETRON
MICROWAVES
TURNTABLE   FOOD

I HEAR A ROOSTER CROWING!

HOW DOES A MICROWAVE OVEN WORK?

Fast. In a microwave oven, a strong electrical current is changed into tiny *micro* waves. These radiate inside the oven, pass right through the food, bounce off the walls, and zip through the food again. The inside and outside are cooked all at once. In a regular oven, heat waves hit the outside of food and slowly cook inward.

WHAT IS THE WORLD'S **LARGEST** LIVING ORGANISM?

A mushroom. You just can't see it. Most of a mushroom plant is underground. The edible part sticks up. (Some are poisonous. *Never* pick and eat a mushroom.) One of the world's largest, called a honey or shoestring fungus, covers 1,500 acres in a Washington State forest. Scientists believe it's 500 to 1,000 years old!

How many languages are there in the world?

About 3,000. And English has the most words. Start increasing your vocabulary because there are over 600,000 words in English plus another 400,000 technical terms. But don't worry, no one knows them all. Even Shakespeare only used about 33,000.

WHY DOES A GIRAFFE HAVE SUCH A LONG NECK?

Animal traits develop over thousands of years. The ones that last are characteristics that help them eat well and avoid enemies. A long neck gives the giraffe two important advantages. It can eat the leaves on the tops of trees that other animals can't reach. And it can see enemies coming from a long way off.

I COULD PLAY PRO BASKETBALL!

Why do I need sleep?

Get up—Go to school—Eat—Run around—Think—Throw a ball. Your body is working all day long. Waste builds up and slows down your systems. It makes you feel tired. Sleep is the time when your body cleans up, repairs, and relaxes. You must sleep. How much? Only your body knows.

WHAT WAS THE ITALIAN RENAISSANCE?

A period of cultural and artistic rebirth that began in Italy in the late 14th century and lasted for roughly 200 years. The Renaissance gradually spread throughout Europe and became the bridge between the medieval and modern worlds. During this revival, people rediscovered the art and learning of Ancient Greece and Rome. Scientists, artists, and philosophers began to consider human beings and their world in a different way—how people felt and what they were really like became important.

In Florence, the ruling Medici family were great supporters of the arts. Their encouragement and financial support led to great achievements by many artists, including Michelangelo and Leonardo DaVinci.

WHO BUILT THE TAJ MAHAL AND WHY?

The magnificent Taj Mahal in northern India is a mausoleum, or tomb, built by the emperor Shah Jahan in memory of his wife. The mausoleum gets its name from *her* name, Mumtaz Mahal, which means "ornament of the palace." Twenty thousand men worked for over 20 years to build the complex, which includes several buildings, a reflecting pool, and a walled garden. The square tomb (186 feet on each side) has white marble walls, decorated with semiprecious stones, and is topped by five marble domes. The building was completed in 1648. Shah Jahan is also buried there.

HOW DO PEANUTS GROW?

Upside down. "Nuts" are really the seeds of the plant they come from. Most plants grow up toward the sun. But not the nutty peanut plant. Its seed pods grow downward and bury themselves in the soil. Then the peanut ripens underground.

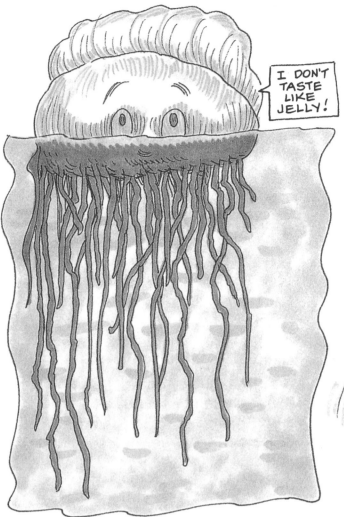

WHAT ARE JELLYFISH?

They're not really fish, because they don't have backbones. Jellyfish are undersea creatures with tentacles and a jelly-like body shaped like an upside down cup. The sting you feel in the water is the poison a jellyfish releases to catch prey. The Portuguese man-of-war has tentacles that can be more than 100 feet long. It can produce very painful stings if touched by a human.

WHY DO MY MUSCLES ACHE WHEN I EXERCISE A LOT?

Bend your elbow, clench your fist, and make a muscle in your arm. Feel the muscle get rounder and firmer? Now let go. Feel it stretch and relax? When you *contract* and *relax* a muscle, the tissues produce lactic acid. That creates the achy, tired feeling you get. Rest, and you're ready to go again.

HOW DO FIREWORKS WORK?

All that dazzle, flash, and sparkle is chemistry in motion. A firecracker is a two-staged event set off by gunpowder, chemicals, and a fuse. Light a firecracker and the gunpowder sends it flying. Then the fuse ignites the chemicals—and pow—strontium burns red; barium, green; copper, blue; and sodium, yellow. But remember, all that beauty is dangerous. Keep your hands *off!*

HOW MUCH DOES MY BRAIN WEIGH?

About 2% of your body weight. That's two pounds if you weigh 100. But the brain needs about ten times more of your body's resources— 20% of the oxygen you breathe, 20% of the calories in the food you eat, and 15% of the blood you have. Your busy brain needs lots of fuel to keep you going.

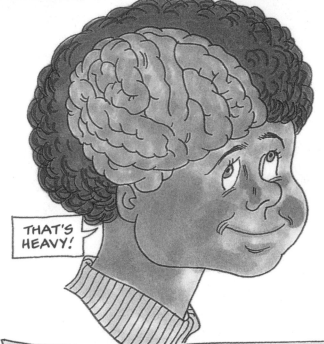

THAT'S HEAVY!

WHICH LANGUAGE IS SPOKEN BY THE MOST PEOPLE IN THE WORLD?

English. But, check the numbers. For many people, English is a second language. Estimates range from 800 million to 1.5 billion English speakers in the world. But English is the *native tongue* of only 350 million. Of those, 220 million live in North America. Mandarin Chinese is the most common *first language*, shared by close to a billion people.

THANK YOU!

SHIEH-SHIEH!

HOW DO MIGRATING BIRDS KNOW WHERE THEY ARE GOING?

They probably follow the same guides used by sailors of ancient times: the stars, the sun, and geographic features such as shorelines and mountains. Some scientists think that birds also use Earth's magnetic fields to help them find their way, but this theory has not been proven. Most migrating birds use specific north-south routes called flyways.

WHO FIRST STARTED USING MAKEUP?

Japanese actors, African dancers, Egyptian princesses, and Roman empresses. Makeup has been around since ancient times. Over two thousand years ago Cleopatra, the queen of Egypt, blackened her upper eyelids and lashes and put dark green color under her eyes. Red was the color of choice for cheeks and lips in Rome. What's new today? Not much—just more brands and colors to choose from.

HOW OFTEN DO TIDES CHANGE?

Four times a day. In any given place, two low tides and two high tides usually occur each day.

The time of each tide varies slightly from day to day. Using knowledge of an area's shoreline, sea depth, and other factors, experts draw up tide charts that list the times of the tides for specific dates. Sailors and other people who live or work near seacoasts use the charts to help them plan anything that would be affected by the water's depth.

HOW MANY BONES ARE IN MY BODY?

Adults have 206. You had about 275 when you were born. As you grow some smaller bones fuse together to form larger, stronger ones. More than half your bones are in your hands and feet. Your thigh bone, or femur, is the largest. The ossicles, inside your ears, are the smallest. Bones protect your organs. And the marrow in the center of bones produces the red and white blood cells you need to live.

Why do camels have humps? How long can a camel go without water?

WILL YOU BRING ME A GLASS OF WATER, PLEASE?

Camels are built for long, dry journeys. Their humps are for fat storage. When food is short, they use up the fat for energy. Their stomach lining is specially built for water storage. How long camels can go without a drink depends on their travel speed and the weight of the load they're carrying. It's about 6 to 10 days if traveling is slow and easy.

Who kept the world's longest diary?

A very old person. Colonel Ernest Loftus, of Zimbabwe, began writing in his diary when he was 12 years old. He kept it up for 91 years until he died in 1987. He was 103.

Why do flowers have such bright colors?

To attract the birds and the bees so the flowers can be pollinated (fertilized) and produce seeds. Most flowers rely on insects and birds to carry their pollen. The visitors brush against the pollen and carry it on their bodies from one part of the flower to another, or from one flower to another.

HOW LONG CAN A SNAKE GET?

If the snake could stand on its tail and you were at a window on the third story of a building, about 30 feet up, the snake could look you in the eye! This long, *long* snake could be an anaconda or a reticulated python, but fortunately, both stick to the ground.

WHO INVENTED SURFING?

People began surfing before anyone thought to record it. Hawaiians were catching waves when Captain Cook discovered the islands in 1778. They used big, heavy boards in those days. When smaller, lightweight boards were invented in the 1930s, surfing took off.

94

SPEED OF LIGHT?

DO YOU WANT TO RACE?

OKAY!

Incredibly fast—faster than anyone can imagine. Light travels at a speed of about 186,000 miles per second. The circumference of the Earth (the distance around the world) is about 24,800 miles. That means light could travel around the world about seven and a half times in a single second!

WHAT INSECT FLIES THE FASTEST?

The dragonfly. When a dragonfly comes by, duck! It can travel as fast as 30 miles per hour. But compared to many insects, this big bug beats its wings slowly— only about 25 to 40 beats per second. When a tiny mosquito takes off, it beats its wings (buzzzz!) about 600 beats per second, but only travels about one mile per hour.

DRAW ME!

Who was Walt Disney?

Mickey Mouse's "father." Disney (1901–1966) was a famous filmmaker. One of his earliest and most well-known creations was Mickey Mouse. In 1928, Mickey starred in Disney's first sound cartoon, *Steamboat Willie*, and Disney was his voice.

Disney created the first full-length cartoon, *Snow White and the Seven Dwarfs*, in 1937. He built Disneyland theme park in California in 1955. Disney World, near Orlando, Florida, was opened in 1971.

Why do plants have thorns?
Why do cacti have needles?

HI, ROSE!

HI, CACTUS!

It's a jungle out there, and plants have to defend themselves. Thorns and needles are the weapons of the plant world. Any animal that takes a bite out of a cactus is *not* coming back for a second helping.

WHAT'S AT THE CENTER OF THE EARTH?

THAT'S HOT!!

Hot stuff. Scientists believe the Earth has four layers. The *crust*, or solid rock, goes down about 20 miles (that's about five miles beneath the oceans). The next layer, the *mantle*, is about 1,800 miles deep. Then we come to the outer core, which is 1,400 miles of hot, liquid rock. And finally, to the core, 800 miles thick, a ball of hot, hot, 12,000 degrees Fahrenheit hot, solid rock.

WHAT ARE SEASHELLS MADE OF?

"Skeletons." Mollusks, like snails and clams, have their skeletons on the outside of their soft bodies instead of on the inside. They are shells—mostly made of limestone, a substance shellfish take from the water and convert into shell material. These skeletons grow as the animals inside them grow. A mollusk is attached to its shell, so if a shell is empty, the animal is gone for good.

WHAT HAPPENS WHEN WATER BOILS?

It disappears. Actually, at 212°Fahrenheit (100°Celsius), water changes to steam, which is a gas. All liquids become gases when heated to a certain point. Heat loosens the bonds between a liquid's molecules, and they spread apart, becoming a light, thin gas. At 32°F (0°C), water's molecules slow down and bind together into solid ice.

IS THAT ONE OF US?

I JUST PROVED THAT THE MOON IS NOT MADE OF CHEESE!!

WHO WAS THE FIRST PERSON TO SET FOOT ON THE MOON?

Neil Armstrong, pilot of *Apollo 11*. On July 20, 1969, he and Buzz Aldrin rode the *Eagle*, a vehicle that detached from the main spacecraft, and landed on an area of the moon called the Sea of Tranquillity. As he put his foot on the moon's surface, he said, "That's one small step for [a] man, one giant leap for mankind."

WHAT IS THE WORLD'S TALLEST MOUNTAIN?

MOUNT EVEREST

Mount Everest in the Himalayas on the border of Tibet and Nepal. It's 29,028 feet high. In 1953, Edmund Hillary and Tenzing Norgay were the first people ever to reach the top. In 1978, Reinhold Messner and Peter Habeler were the first to succeed without using bottled oxygen. The air gets very thin up there and breathing is difficult.

Why does a year have 365 days?

The number of days in the year is based on the sun. A solar day is the length of time it takes the Earth to rotate on its axis one time. A solar year is the number of solar days it takes for the Earth to revolve around the sun once. That number is exactly 365 days, 5 hours, 48 minutes, and 46 seconds. This explains leap years, which have 366 days. After four years, those extra five or so hours add up to a full day.

Who was Alexander the Great?

Alexander the Great got his name the hard way. He fought for it. Alexander was born in 356 B.C. and was only 20 years old when he became ruler of Macedonia, which is north of Greece. He set out to conquer the world and built an empire as big as the United States. It extended from Greece to Egypt and as far east as India. And he did it all in 13 years! Alexander died when he was only 33.

HOW HOT DOES LIGHTNING GET?

Very hot indeed: up to 54,000 degrees Fahrenheit! That is more than five times as hot as the surface of the sun. Lightning is also very "hot" in another way: A single bolt of lightning has 30 million volts of electricity—enough energy to power New York City!

That makes lightning dangerous. If you get caught in a thunderstorm, take shelter. One of the safest places to be is in a car with the windows rolled up. Don't try to outrun the storm: a lightning bolt travels at about 60,000 miles *per second*!

Why did the dinosaurs die out?

Dinosaurs lived on the Earth for so long (about 160 million years!) and so successfully that scientists aren't sure why they died out. There are plenty of theories. A heat wave: changes in the Earth's climate may have made it too hot for plants and animals. A cold front: the dust from crashing meteorites could have blocked out the sun. Sunburn: volcanoes could have burnt through the Earth's protective ozone layer, letting through deadly ultraviolet radiation. Other theories say the extinctions were due to disease, sea-level changes, shifting continents, and mammals that ate dinosaur eggs. Which answer is right? We may never know for sure.

Why do dolphins seem smart?

They're brainy. A dolphin's brain, in relation to its body size, is as big as a human's. But the dolphin brain is much simpler than the human brain. Dolphins are naturally curious and playful. They learn quickly and even understand some language. Because this behavior seems "human," we think of dolphins as being smart—and, in their way, they are.

WHAT'S THE SMELLIEST THING IN THE WORLD?

There are thousands of smells in the world and millions of opinions on what is the worst. The cause of a nasty smell is its chemical combination. For example, rotten eggs could be one of the smelliest things in the world. The odor is from sulfur dioxide. As for the chemical ethyl mercaptan, if you ever came across it you wouldn't forget it. It is said to smell like a combination of rotting cabbage, garlic, onions, burned toast, and sewer gas.

HOW DO WAVES FORM IN THE OCEAN?

Waves start with wind, not water. Picture the wind moving across the surface of the ocean, lifting the water. When the wind blows harder, the waves get bigger. When the winds are calm, waves are usually no more than a few feet high. But in a storm, they may be whipped up to 60 feet tall. One of the highest waves recorded in the Pacific Ocean was 112 feet high—a wall of water taller than a 10-story building!

WHO WAS HOUDINI?

The greatest escape artist of all time. Harry Houdini (1874–1926) was a magician who created contraptions of ropes, handcuffs, tires, and chains from which only he could escape. He was nailed inside boxes. He was trapped in water-filled tanks. He was wrapped up in a straight-jacket and dropped in the ocean. But he always got free.

HOW DOES A ROCKET SOUND IN SPACE?

Like one hand clapping—there's no sound at all. Sound is created by "sound waves," a movement of the molecules that make up air. In space there is no air. Therefore, there are no waves and no sound.

How does a firefighter put out a fire?

As quickly as possible—and it depends on the fire. Any fire must have fuel, heat, and oxygen. A wood, paper, or fabric fire is put out with powerful streams of water, which absorb the heat. But water can't put out an electrical fire because it conducts electricity. And water doesn't mix with oil, grease, or gas, so it's not useful for those fires. Grease and electrical fires are snuffed out with carbon dioxide, which cuts off the fire's oxygen. Gas fires are fought with water fog, a spray of fine water particles, and foam. These form a blanket over the fire and smother it.

What is a vaccine?

Medications that cause a person's body to develop resistance, or immunity, to a particular disease. Certain illnesses--like chicken pox, measles, or polio--are known to make people very sick. By giving a person a small amount of the virus from a disease, the body will fight it and grow cells that will "remember" the virus and attack it any time it tries to infect the body again. We now have vaccines for many illnesses. Some are so successful that certain diseases have been eliminated from parts of the world where everyone is vaccinated.

CAN I GET PEOPLE POX?

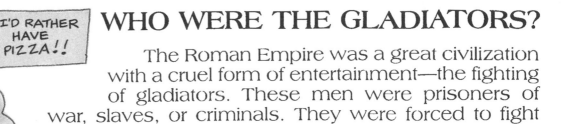

WHO WERE THE GLADIATORS?

The Roman Empire was a great civilization with a cruel form of entertainment—the fighting of gladiators. These men were prisoners of war, slaves, or criminals. They were forced to fight each other in a great stadium while the Romans cheered. Most of the time, the gladiators battled until one gruesomely killed the other. These fights were usually part of festivals that sometimes went on for months. All this "fun" lasted from 264 B.C. to A.D. 404.

WHAT MAKES A DIAMOND SPARKLE?

You can't have sparkle without light, and diamonds make the most of it. A diamond is a pure carbon crystal formed beneath the earth under severe heat and pressure. But it doesn't sparkle in its natural form. Diamond cutters cut *facets*—small surfaces—into the stone that catch the light. A cut diamond has the ability to bend the light and reflect it more than any other substance, and that makes it sparkle.

Which U.S. president spent the most time in office?

FDR: Franklin Delano Roosevelt. Our 32nd president, he was elected four times and was president for 12 years. Roosevelt's administration led the U.S. out of the Great Depression, established the first Social Security Act, and guided the U.S. through most of World War II, which ended shortly after he died in office. Although not many citizens knew it at the time, Roosevelt was largely confined to a wheelchair due to the polio he contracted as a young man. After Franklin Roosevelt's death, a law was passed limiting U.S. presidents from serving more than two terms.

What are spittlebugs?

Not too many bugs are a pretty sight, but spittle-bugs are stuck with an ugly name. "Spittle" is a word for the bubbly saliva mess we all think of as "spit." Spittlebugs are small jumping insects, less than half an inch long, that look like tiny frogs. In their *nymph*, or infant stage, they live in a frothy, spittlelike mass, which they create themselves. So "spittlebug," after all, is a name they deserve.

WHY DO WE GET GOOSE BUMPS?

When we get cold, the hairs on our body stand up straight. When this happens, our skin pushes up into little bumps. Our body may be trying to keep us warm, but the hairs we have just don't do the trick! If we had fur or feathers that stood on end, the air between them would hold in the heat and keep the cold out. So, unfortunately, we remain cold and simply look like geese whose feathers have just been plucked.

WHO INVENTED ICE CREAM?

It remains a mystery. Most historians agree that Italy's Catherine de Medici, with help from chef Bernardo Buontalenti, introduced "cream ice" to France in 1533. The cold, creamy confection wasn't known as "ice cream" until it reached America in the 1700s, where it became wildly popular. First president George Washington spent a great deal of money on the expensive dessert. He even liked to make it at home with a "Cream Machine for Making Ice." The price dropped a century later when Jacob Fussell, a Baltimore dairyman, invented the first ice-cream factory.

WHY IS 13

CONSIDERED AN UNLUCKY NUMBER?

Poor number 13. People have been uneasy about it since primitive humans counted their ten fingers and two feet and came up with 12. After that came the unknown—13. And anything unknown is scary. As with all superstitions, there is no reasonable answer. But that doesn't mean people don't take it seriously. Many hotels and office buildings don't have a 13th floor!

What happens to bears when they hibernate?

Not much. When most animals hibernate, their body temperature drops and their breathing slows down. Not bears. They just sleep away most of the winter in a normal, but very drowsy, state. Cubs are born in the winter, and the mothers practically sleep through the whole ordeal! Everyone may get up and walk around for awhile, but then it's back to the den to sleep until spring.

DO NOT DISTURB

Z-Z-Z-Z

Has anyone ever found pirate's treasure?

Yes! More than 100,000 objects were recovered from the *Whydah*, a ship captured in 1717 by the pirate Samuel Bellamy off the coast of the Bahamas. The shipwrecked vessel was *salvaged*, or brought up from the sea, in 1984. Among the treasures was a collection of gold jewelry, created by the Akan people of Africa.

WHAT IS AIR MADE OF?

It feels like nothing, but air is definitely something. It's invisible, but it's not weightless. Air is made up of gases, mostly nitrogen and some oxygen with a small amount of argon. There's also a bit of water vapor. A hundred miles of air rises above your head—or sits on your shoulders.

DOES A CAT REALLY HAVE NINE LIVES?

It just seems that way. Cats are fast and flexible—and they have an excellent sense of balance. They bound out of the way of danger. They fall from scary heights and land on their feet. They squeeze out of tight spots. Cats escape harm so often that people say they have "nine lives."

106

WHY DO FLIES HAVE SUCH BIG EYES?

"The better to see you with, my dear." Most insects have large eyes made up of many lenses. These are called *compound eyes.* (Some dragonflies have 300,000 lenses in each eye!) In fact, flies don't see too clearly because each lens is fixed and can't be adjusted for distance. But flies with eyes that cover most of their heads have 360-degree vision. They can see anything coming at them from any-where—which is why it's so hard to catch a fly.

THIS MUST BE HEAVEN!!

NO BALL PLAYING ALLOWED

What happens to the garbage I throw away?

All 1,300 pounds? That's about how much garbage each one of us throws away every year. Some solid waste goes into landfills. These are low areas where towns build mountains of garbage. The piles are packed down and covered with dirt. Very slowly, over years, tiny living organisms called microbes break down the garbage and it decays. Some solid waste is burned in huge furnaces called incinerators. Other garbage can be *recycled*. Metal objects, such as cans, are crushed, shredded, cleaned, and melted. Then the metal is recycled, or used again. Newspapers, bottles, and plastics are also recycled.

NOBODY WANTS TO PLAY WITH ME!

Are all sharks dangerous?

No—but never test a shark to find out. Fewer than a hundred people worldwide are attacked by sharks each year. Twenty kinds of sharks have been known to attack people, and a few others are considered dangerous. Whale sharks are the most friendly. They can weigh more than 30,000 pounds, but they're so gentle, sometimes divers hold on to their fins and take a ride.

A WAVE IS NICE BUT... BANANAS ARE BETTER!

HOW CAN APES LEARN SIGN LANGUAGE ?

I GET TO CELEBRATE BOTH FATHER'S AND MOTHER'S DAY!

Do male animals ever give birth?

Male sea horses do—sort of. The female sea horse lays her eggs into a pouch on the male's stomach. He carries the eggs and, after they hatch, carries the young for about six weeks. Then, by contracting his pouch, he pushes out a bunch of young sea horses.

WHAT'S THE DIFFERENCE BETWEEN A MOTH AND A BUTTERFLY?

Night flight: Moths fly mostly at dark and butterflies during the day. *Antennae:* Butterflies have long, knob-tipped antennae and moths have feathery ones. *Body shape:* Butterflies are slim and moths are chunky. However, if you pick up either by the wings, you may get a fine dust on your fingers. These are the scales that prove that, despite their differences, both belong to the same group of "scaly-winged" creatures, the Lepidoptera.

Apes learn sign language based on the hand signals that deaf people use. The apes watch their trainer's hands, imitate the movements, and get a reward when they get it right. Apes can even put two signs together to make a phrase, such as "Want food." Using sign language they can also "talk" to each other. There are several apes that have learned to sign. Kanzi, a bonobo, or pygmy chimpanzee, knows 660 signs. But Koko, a gorilla who died in 2000, knew over 1,000 signs. She was ape with a lot to say!

What happens when a space shuttle returns to Earth's atmosphere?

It's a hot moment. When the shuttle enters Earth's atmosphere, gravity takes hold and the surrounding air causes enormous friction. Friction causes heat. In this case, the fiery temperature is more than we can imagine—3,000°F. The shuttle is protected by special tiles on its underside. They are so good at shedding heat that they can be burning hot on one side and cool enough to touch on the other.

WHY DOES A BOOMERANG COME BACK?

I JUST CAN'T SEEM TO THROW IT AWAY!!!

It's all in your wrist and the boomerang's arms.

Boomerang arms are curved on top and flat on the bottom, like airplane wings. The wind rushing over them creates "lift," and causes it to "fly" forward. But only one arm points away from the wind, creating lift in the other direction. With a good snap of the wrist, a boomerang spins very quickly. This combination of spinning and opposite lift curves its flight, guiding the boomerang back to its thrower.

Who was Michelangelo?

One of the great artists of the Italian Renaissance. Michelangelo Buonarroti, born in 1475, had many talents. He was a sculptor, painter, architect, and poet who created some of the most spectacular works of all time. He is best known for painting the biblical scenes on the ceiling of the Sistine Chapel in the Vatican—sometimes lying on his back to paint! Other great works include his 14-foot-tall statue, *David*, and the design of the dome of St. Peter's church in Rome.

WHAT IS A SLOTH?

A slow-moving, furry mammal that lives in the tropical forests of Central and South America. It lives in the trees—eating, sleeping, and maneuvering upside down, clinging with sharp claws. Sloths rarely move faster than six feet a minute. If they do come down from a tree, they only hurry—well, sort of—to another tree.

Who created the first zoo?

The first zoo was created in the twelfth century B.C. by King Wen of China. It was called *The Garden of Intelligence*. He collected different animals from across his empire to live in his zoo. Today, the best zoos want their animals to feel at home, so they create environments similar to an animal's natural surroundings. A zoo also helps to save animals that are in danger of extinction.

WHAT ARE THE SEVEN WONDERS OF THE ANCIENT WORLD?

> Amazing human-made structures, most of which no longer exist.

Tombs of pharaohs were built around 2600 B.C. by thousands of laborers. The **Great Pyramid of Khufu**, in Giza, Egypt, is the largest of these, covering about 13 acres and standing 482 feet high. One of the Seven Ancient Wonders, it is the only one surviving today.

The **Hanging Gardens of Babylon** were built around 600 B.C.for the queen of Babylon. The ancient city of Babylon was located close to where Baghdad, Iraq, is today. Early writings tell us that the gardens were laid out on a 300-square-foot brick terrace about 76 feet above the ground. Laborers worked around the clock to lift water from the Euphrates River to water the flowers.

WHO MOWS THE LAWN?

The **Temple of Artemis at Ephesus** was built around 550 B.C.in the Greek city of Ephesus to honor the goddess Artemis. All marble, it was one of the most complicated temples ever built in ancient times. It had 127 columns, each 60 feet high.

The Colossus of Rhodes was a huge bronze statue in the city of Rhodes in ancient Greece. It was built to honor Helios, the sun god. It took 12 years to complete and was probably 120 feet tall, about the same size as the Statue of Liberty. In 224 B.C., the statue was destroyed by an earthquake.

The Statue of Zeus was built around 435 B.C. in Olympia, Greece. Zeus was the king of the gods in ancient Greece—and this statue fit his role. It was said to be 40 feet high. Zeus was carved in ivory sitting on his throne in royal robes made of gold.

The Mausoleum at Halicarnassus was built around 353 B.C. in what is now Turkey. The marble tomb was constructed for Mausolus, an official of the Persian Empire. The tomb became so famous that large tombs are now called *mausoleums*.

The Lighthouse of Alexandria was on the island of Pharos in the harbor of Alexandria, Egypt. Built in 270 B.C., it was said to be more than 440 feet high, square on the bottom, eight-sided in the middle, and circular on top—where a fire burned to guide ships at night.

IT'S A GIRL

How **big** is a baby whale?

Bigger than any other baby on Earth. The largest whale is the blue whale and its baby is the biggest. At birth, these babies can be 20 to 26 feet long and weigh more than 6,000 pounds. Just one year later they can grow to 28 tons!

HOW DOES REMOTE CONTROL WORK?

Invisibly—with infrared light rays and electricity. If you want to change the channel on your TV, you press a button on the remote control unit and send a beam of infrared rays to the receiver unit in the TV. The beam contains a signal made up of electrical pulses. The receiver detects the signal. Then it "decodes" the signal and changes the channel.

WHO INVENTED CHEWING GUM?

The stuff of "chewing" gum is chicle (CHEE-clay), the gum of the sapodilla tree. The Aztec Indians of Mexico chewed it to clean their teeth. In 1872, Thomas Adams mixed sugar and flavor with chicle and created a rubbery candy. Actually, he was looking for a substitute for rubber when he popped a piece of chicle into his mouth. He chewed on his idea for a while and out popped gum!

ZAP!

CAN HAIL FALL IN HOT WEATHER?

Yes, as long as the air high above is cold enough. Some of the biggest hailstones have fallen during summer thunderstorms, when rain droplets were frozen and refrozen in the supercooled air sweeping through high storm clouds. In fact, the largest hailstone ever recorded in the U.S. fell in early summer. On June 22, 2003, a hailstone measuring 18.75 inches around, and probably weighing over a pound, fell at Aurora, Nebraska.

OH, NO! HAIL!!

What makes a flower smell good?

All plants and animals have characteristics or behaviors that help them reproduce. In order to grow seeds, flowers must transfer pollen from their male parts to their female parts. Insects often carry the pollen, and flowers attract insects with their smells. The perfume comes from tiny particles called scent strips, on the petals and other parts of the flower.

OUCH!

Does it hurt a woodpecker to hammer on a tree?

No. Woodpeckers are hard-headed. They have thick skulls that can take the banging, and strong neck muscles that absorb the shock. Woodpeckers drill holes to get at the insects inside trees.

When did women first compete in the Olympic Games?

Women first competed in the Olympic Games in golf and tennis in 1900. They wore long skirts, which certainly didn't help their game. As time went on, women began competing in almost all the sports that men have been playing for centuries.

WHAT IS VIRTUAL REALITY?

Reality is reading this book. Or sitting in a chair. Or anything that happens to you. Virtual Reality (VR, for short) is not real life, but it can be close. People create VR with computers. They feed the computer information. The computer turns the facts into visual images that behave and move as if they were real. To "feel" the virtual world, you might wear a headset or goggles, a computerized vest, or a pair of gloves. Your chair might be attached to the computer. If you were on a roller coaster in virtual reality, you would feel the sensations of the ride. You would be plunged into a new "unreal" reality.

HOW DOES A TADPOLE TURN INTO A FROG?

Metamorphosis (met-ah-MORE-foh-sis). That's the big word for change in an animal's body. Frogs begin life as tadpoles—tiny, tailed, fishlike creatures that breathe with gills in the water. As tadpoles grow, rear legs appear, then front legs. Then the tail disappears and the creature *looks* like a frog. But it is not until lungs replace the gills that the tadpole *becomes* a frog— an animal that breathes air on land. Some frogs metamorphose in days or weeks. The big, noisy bullfrog takes nearly a year.

DO ANY REAL HAUNTED HOUSES EXIST?

It's spooky, but many people think they do. The Winchester House in California is a big house actually built for ghosts. Sarah Winchester, heiress to the Winchester rifle fortune, was told by a psychic that a curse had been placed on her by the ghosts of people killed by the rifles. To get rid of the curse, the psychic told Sarah to build a house for the spirits. At the end of 38 years the house had 160 rooms and 950 doors! In her will, Sarah insisted that ghosts always be welcomed there. Want to visit?

WE'LL TAKE IT!

FOR RENT

WHAT MAKES SPECIAL EFFECTS ON TV AND IN THE MOVIES SO REAL?

PUFF!

Cinematography. Camera techniques used in movies create illusions—scenes that look real, but are not. One technique is "rear screen projection." A separate film is shown behind the actors so they appear to be in a scene, but they really aren't. Another trick is to film tiny figures so that they look life-size. Imagine a doll-size plastic dragon and a model boat in a bucket of water. Look again. The camera makes it seem like a monster rising out of the ocean to attack a ship. That's entertainment!

What are feathers made of?

Keratin, a protein, the same substance that you have in your hair and nails. Feathers on a bird are called plumage, and they can be beautiful colors—red, yellow, brown, even blue and violet. But they're not just for decoration. Feathers are for flying.

I'M REALLY BEAUTIFUL!

I'M EVERMORE BEAUTIFUL!

NO, I'M BEAUTIFUL!

I'M THE MOST BEAUTIFUL!

I'M BEAUTIFUL!

HOW DO I REMEMBER THINGS?

Think of your brain as a gigantic computer, but much more complicated. Nerve cells take in information and pass it back and forth. Suppose you eat a peach for the first time. Nerves in your eyes, nose, and mouth pass along news to your brain about how a peach looks, smells, and tastes. Your brain records the word "peach" and the experience of eating it. The next time you think of a peach your brain will call up the stored information.

I'M A KING!

I'M A QUEEN!

I'M A ROOK!

I'M A KNIGHT!

I'M A PAWN!

I'M A BISHOP!

WHO INVENTED CHESS?

The earliest recorded chess games were played in Persia about 1,500 years ago. The term "checkmate" comes from the Persian phrase *shah mat*, which means "the king cannot escape." The Arabs learned chess when they conquered Persia in the seventh century A.D., and then brought the game to Spain, from where it spread throughout Europe. International tournaments began in 1851.

WHERE IS THE RING OF FIRE?

Where the volcanoes are. The Ring of Fire describes the area where more than 75 percent of the world's 850 active volcanoes are. The boundaries are where the earth's crust under the Pacific Ocean meets the continents. The "ring" goes from Alaska in North America to Chile in South America on one side and from Siberia to New Zealand on the other. The most volcanoes are in Indonesia—a very hot spot.

I'M FEELING MIGHTY OLD!

How long can an insect live?

Although most of the over 2,500 species of cicadas around the world have life spans of two to five years, one North American species lives up to 17 years. After cicadas mate, the females deposit eggs (hundreds of them!) in trees. The adult insects then die within weeks. When the eggs hatch, the nymphs, as they're called, fall to the earth and burrow into the ground over a foot deep. After either 13 or 17 years (it varies), the nymphs of these long-living cicadas surface and complete their transformation into adult insects. Then as adults, they begin the whole process again. But cicadas are only teenagers compared to termite queens. Some queens can live up to 50 years!

119

HOW MANY GALAXIES ARE IN THE UNIVERSE?

8 BILLION
AND 2...
8 BILLION
AND 3...
8 BILLION
AND 4...

Billions—more than we can see with even the most powerful telescopes. Each galaxy is a huge collection of gas, dust, and, probably, billions of stars, all held together by gravity. The sun and its planets, including Earth, are part of a galaxy called the Milky Way. Look for a hazy band of bright stars across the night sky and you may see part of it.

How did the U.S. acquire Alaska?

It was a purchase from Russia. In 1866 U.S. Secretary of State William Seward made a deal with the Russian minister to the United States. Russia needed money, and the U.S. needed more room to expand (at least that's what William Seward thought). He was finally able to convince President Andrew Johnson to support his efforts and in 1868 the United States paid 7.2 million dollars to Russia for the territory. Many U.S. legislators thought it was a wasteful expense and called the transaction "Seward's Folly." That was shortly before large amounts of gold were discovered in the region . . . and long before valuable oil reserves were found!

BURP!

EXCUSE ME!

WHY DO WE BURP?

It's the body's way of getting rid of the air we "eat." When you take a big gulp of food, you're treating your stomach to air along with it. When you drink a fizzy soda, those air-filled bubbles bounce around in your belly. Sometimes the entrance valve to the stomach opens and the air rushes up. It vibrates in the throat and makes the noise we call—excuse me—a burp.

Who was the first African American to play baseball in the major leagues?

Jackie Robinson, a real sports hero. When he began playing for the Brooklyn Dodgers in 1947, he was the only African American in baseball. Unfortunately, there were still a lot of people who thought he didn't belong. But he stood up for what was right. He played for 10 years and helped his team win six National League pennants. In 1962, Jackie Robinson became the first African American to enter the National Baseball Hall of Fame.

WHAT IS DÉJÀ VU?

ƧUV ÁLÈG ƧI TAHW

Have you ever been someplace for the first time but had the feeling you'd been there before? Have you ever met a stranger and felt like you'd met him or her before? This odd feeling is called déjà vu. The word comes from the French *déjà*, which means "already," plus *vu*, which means "seen."

Who was William Shakespeare?

The greatest writer of the English language. William Shakespeare, or the Bard of Avon, as he was called, lived in England from 1564 to 1616. He grew up in Stratford-upon-Avon where he studied Latin and Greek Classics at the local grammar school until age 14. Unlike the other writers and playwrights of his day, he had no university education. Yet he became immensely successful writing and publishing sonnets (14-line poems) and plays—154 sonnets and 37 plays, including Romeo and Juliet and Hamlet. He was a favorite of Queen Elizabeth I, and his theatre company regularly performed at court.

WHO MADE THE FIRST MAP?

Someone who wasn't going too far. The first known map was a clay tablet that shows a portion of the Euphrates River in Mesopotamia, which is now Iraq. That was around 2300 B.C. The most famous ancient maps were made by Claudius Ptolemy, an Egyptian scholar. Around A.D. 150 he drew a map of the world as it was known at that time. He included regional maps of Europe, Africa, and Asia. The whole Western Hemisphere was yet to be discovered. In other words, we weren't on the map.

What was Mark Twain's real name?

Samuel Clemens. One of America's greatest writers, he lived from 1835 to 1910, and his books are just as much fun today as they were a century ago. Two of his stories, *The Adventures of Tom Sawyer* and *The Adventures of Huckleberry Finn*, are among the best-known novels in American fiction.

WHEN WAS THE FIRST BOOK PRINTED?

The first book was "printed" in China in A.D. 868 with wooden blocks dipped in ink. Other wooden block systems were invented, but they were too slow and difficult to use to create many books. In 15th-century Germany, Johannes Gutenberg invented a way to print with metal blocks that moved around and could be used again and again. In 1455, with this first printing press, he produced copies of the Gutenberg Bible. For the first time, books were available to many people.

What is HDTV?

HDTV—or High Definition TV—is the digital format used to create the ultra-clear images on television sets today. Older TV sets show a picture that's made of about 210,000 pixels, which are like tiny dots of visual information. But HDTV formats show images made up of about 2 million pixels! That's why HDTV images are really clear, with better color and more detail than old TV's have. Watching HDTV is almost like being at a movie theatre!

What do whale sharks eat?

OOPS!!

THAT'S A WHALE OF A SHARK!

COMING THROUGH!

What happens to the water I drink?

GULP!

WHO INVENTED CHEESE?

It goes to work. About half your blood is made up of water, which moves blood cells through your veins and arteries. Water also plays a big role in your organs. For example, water in your liver helps process digested foods. Water in your kidneys helps filter waste out of your blood, and water in your urine carries the waste out of your body. A grown man has 10 quarts of water circulating in his body every day.

Cheese is an ancient food. Experts believe that it was first eaten in the Middle East. It seems likely that someone who raised cows, goats, or sheep first made cheese by accident. When milk sours, it separates into curds (soft clumps) and whey (liquid). Curds can be aged into cheese. The Sumerians, a people who thrived 6,000 years ago in the area that is now Iraq, were probably the world's first cheese lovers.

Whale sharks are the world's biggest fish, but that's no reason to fear them. These gentle giants don't eat people—just tiny sea life. A whale shark uses its thousands of tiny teeth to eat small plants, shrimp, and fish.

WHY DO THE DAYS GET LONGER AND SHORTER DURING THE YEAR?

Because we're spinning. Earth spins, or rotates, tilted on its *axis*, an imaginary line from the North Pole to the South Pole. Earth also makes a complete orbit around the sun each year. These two motions constantly put us in different positions relative to the sun. During part of the year, the North Pole tilts toward the sun, causing longer days in the Northern Hemisphere. When the South Pole tilts toward the sun, the Southern Hemisphere has longer days. This happens gradually, as Earth's position shifts. So each day, the amount of light reaching your part of the world changes just slightly.

Why did castles have moats?

It was one more way to keep enemies out! During the Middle Ages, landowners in Europe fought over their territory. These "land lords" built their castles as forts, with high stone walls for protection. To keep enemies from climbing the walls, the castle was surrounded by a moat—a deep ditch usually filled with water. A moat was crossed by a drawbridge that could be raised or lowered from within the castle.

What is an ENDANGERED animal?

If an animal species is close to extinction and there are very few left in the world, it is said to be endangered. An animal becomes endangered for many reasons. Pollution may ruin its territory. Cutting down forests may destroy its habitat. Hunting may wipe out its population. Chemicals may poison its food source. But people can make a big difference. In 1987, there were only 27 California Condors left. Conservationists captured and bred the rare birds in an attempt to recover their population. As of 2007, there were more than 300 California Condors. Through conservation efforts, many other endangered animals have been rescued, including the bald eagle, the bison, and the American alligator.

Why does it hurt to pull your hair but not to cut it?

SNIP! SNIP! SNIP!

The hair on your head is dead. Each hair starts growing below the skin in a follicle that contains a root. New cells in the root divide and force older cells upward. That's when the older hair cells die and harden into the hair you see on your head. The hair below the skin is alive and surrounded by nerves. Pull it and you'll feel it!

What is the coldest place on Earth?

About 800 miles from the South Pole in Antarctica. That's where the lowest temperature has been recorded. In July 1983, on a day when you might have been swimming, the temperature in Vostok was -129°F. Don't even think about the wind chill factor!

MOM DID TELL ME TO BUNDLE UP!

What causes an avalanche?

The wind can trigger an avalanche, but so can an earthquake, or melting snow, or a sudden loud sound like a rifle shot. The rest is all downhill—tons of snow, ice, mud, or rock crashing down a mountainside. The wind created by an avalanche can be enormous. In 1970, an avalanche in Peru swept through towns and villages, killing at least 18,000 people on its way.

FEET, DO YOUR THING!!

Which famous composer of music was deaf?

Ludwig van Beethoven (1770–1827)—one of the greatest composers who ever lived. Even as a young German boy his talents were recognized by major artists. He began to lose his hearing at age 30, and his world was silent by age 47. But he kept right on composing, and left the world the gift of his music.

WHAT DOES IT MEAN TO BE DOUBLE-JOINTED?

Nothing. Every elbow, knee, ankle, and shoulder is a spot where two bones meet and a joint connects them. Fingers and toes have many joints. Some people can bend these joints in pretty amazing ways. But they've got the same amount of joints as the rest of us. They're just more flexible.

HOW DOES MY HEART WORK?

Automatically—and it never gets tired. Your heart is a powerful muscle that pumps blood around your body. It's made up of two types of muscle, *striated* (voluntary) and *smooth* (involuntary). Smooth muscle allows the heart to beat regularly. Blood travels through veins and arteries to and from your heart. Arteries carry oxygen-rich blood to every part of your body. Veins carry blood back to your heart to pick up more oxygen. As your heart does its job, the cycle occurs over and over again.

ARTERIES TO HEAD, ARMS, AND NECK

PULMONARY ARTERY

AORTA

SUPERIOR VENA CAVA

VALVE

LEFT ATRIUM

LEFT VENTRICLE

RIGHT PULMONARY VEINS

RIGHT ATRIUM

INFERIOR VENA CAVA

RIGHT VENTRICLE

SEPTUM

IT DOESN'T LOOK LIKE A HEART!

Why do we blink?

To keep our eyes clean. Tear glands under our upper eyelids make tears all the time. When we blink, thousands of times a day, we spread the tears to wash away dust and dirt. Our eyelashes also keep things from entering our eyes. But we can also blink on purpose, as if to say "Just kidding!" That's called winking!

HA-HA-H
HO-HO
HEE-HE

HO-HO-HO
HEE-HEE-HE

WHY DID THE CHICKEN CROSS THE ROAD?

WHY DO WE LAUGH?

Because it feels good and helps us relax. What we laugh at is another story. You could giggle yourself silly over something that your friend thinks is stupid or boring or even insulting. But once you get started, it's hard to stop. Laughter is one of the automatic responses your body takes care of on its own. Your stomach tenses up. Your face scrunches up. Tears squeeze out of your tear glands. And when it's over, you feel good!

How do we grow?

Slowly. Our pituitary gland, located at the bottom of the brain, sets the pace. One of the hormones, or chemicals, it releases stimulates growth, causing our cells to divide and multiply. The more cells there are, the more of us there is! Scientists aren't sure why we stop growing, but fortunately there seems to be a limit.

129

What's the difference between a ROCK and a MINERAL?

A rock is solid material made up of minerals. A mineral forms from chemical combinations in the earth. Salt is one type of mineral. Minerals may be hard or soft, shiny or dull. They may be colorful, and they may conduct heat or electricity. Minerals in different combinations form different types of rocks. Marble, a very hard rock, and chalk, a soft powdery substance, both contain the same mineral—calcium carbonate.

What causes freckles?

Melanin, a naturally occurring brown substance, or *pigment*, found in everybody's skin. The amount of melanin we have determines our skin color. But sometimes our pigment cells produce melanin in clusters. We call these freckles.

Who invented the teddy bear?

I WAS NAMED AFTER HIM!

In 1902, President Teddy Roosevelt went hunting and refused to shoot a bear cub. A cartoonist drew a picture for a newspaper of the great president sparing the life of the little bear. Morris Michtom, a Brooklyn toy maker, thought the cartoon would help him sell stuffed bears. He was right. He put the bear in his window with the picture and called it "Teddy's Bear." Toys in America haven't been the same since. Presidents have come and gone, a century has passed, and the teddy bear is still going strong.

WHERE DO PIÑATAS COME FROM?

South of the border, from Central and South America. Piñatas filled with candy or toys are now found at children's parties all over the world. Often made of papier-mâché in the shape of an animal, piñatas are colorfully decorated and hung from a rope. The idea is to whack the piñata open with a stick or a bat. Sometimes the children are blindfolded, so the treats that spill out are really a surprise.

MISSED!

I'LL GET IT... I'LL GET IT!!

Do animals dream? Do babies?

Babies do, and they spend much more time dreaming than adults. One theory is that we dream to sort out new experiences, knitting them in with the rest of our lives. Babies have a new experience about every minute.

Animals, however, are a different matter. The brains of animals such as reptiles and fish are constructed much differently from ours, making them very difficult to study. But there have been experiments with other mammals, such as monkeys and cats, which seem to show that they dream. Just imagine if they could tell us what they dream about!

SHHH! BE QUIET!

131

WHY DOES THE SUN SHINE?

Because it's big—864,000 miles across—and it's HOT! The sun's core is hotter than you can imagine—about 30,000,000°F. *Thermonuclear* explosions, occurring at the sun's core, create heat and pressure that change hydrogen gas into helium. That process, called *fusion*, creates huge amounts of energy that burst to the surface, appearing as heat and light. This heat and light "shine" all the way to Earth, over 92 million miles away. It takes sunlight about eight minutes to get here.

AH! THAT FEELS GOOD!

I CAN'T EVEN FLY A KITE!

What would it be like to live on the MOON?

You'd be trapped in a space suit because there's no oxygen to breathe. The temperature on the moon ranges from scorching hot, a sizzling 216°F, to the ultimate frozen zone, -279°F! And one cycle from day to night is 27 Earth days.

How does a seed grow into a plant?

Germination—that's a big word for the sprouting of a seed. Seeds need the right temperature, moisture, and oxygen to germinate. First, water softens the seed coat, and the growing parts break out of the seed. A root grows downward. Then the stem bends upward and breaks through the soil. Small roots branch off the main root. Then the leaves develop and the plant is on its own.

Who was King Midas?

In Greek mythology, the god Dionysus gave Midas the ability to turn everything he touched into gold. But there was one problem—even his food turned to gold. Luckily, Dionysus took back his blessing. But the memory of Midas lives on in this saying about successful people: "They have the Midas touch."

THE SUN FEELS GOOD TO ME TOO!

WHAT HAPPENED DURING THE ICE AGES?

THIS IS MY KIND OF AGE!

Ice covered large parts of the Earth. Scientists believe that ice ages occur every 150 million years or so due to changes in the global climate. During the last Ice Age, which ended about 10,000 years ago, parts of North America and Europe were covered with ice up to 9,800 feet thick! Glaciers, huge masses of moving ice, crushed forests, created mountains, and carved out valleys. As the global climate warmed, glaciers began to melt and receded toward the North and South Poles. Glaciers still exist in cold parts of the world, such as Greenland, Canada, and Antarctica.

Who was Joan of Arc?

A French farm girl who became a saint by fighting for her country. Jeanne d'Arc (1412–1431) lived at a time when France was at war with England and losing badly. Jeanne had visions that convinced her she could liberate France. She persuaded the king to allow her to lead men into battle—imagine a 17-year-old girl in armor giving orders to generals! She recaptured the city of Orléans and became a great hero. In the end, she was captured by her enemies and burned at the stake as a witch. In 1920, the Roman Catholic Church declared her a saint.

What's the difference between KARATE and TAE KWON DO?

Both are martial arts, Asian forms of unarmed combat. Karate developed in Okinawa, Japan, in the 17th century. Tae Kwon Do began in Korea around 50 B.C. Karate means "empty hand" and focuses on using the hands and arms. Tae Kwon Do means "the art of kicking and punching" and focuses more on leg power. Aside from self-defense and physical fitness, all martial arts set out to teach a way of life. Emphasis is on concentration, confidence, and harmony with nature. Fighting is the last option for solving a conflict in real life.

Where is the world's longest roller

IS EARTH THE ONLY PLANET THAT HAS A MOON?

I'M NOT THE ONLY ONE!

Heavens, no! In our solar system the planets circle the sun. Moons circle most of the planets—and that's many moons. Saturn has at least 22, and Jupiter has at least 16. Uranus is right up there with at least 15 moons, and Neptune follows with 8 or more. Only Mercury and Venus are out there alone.

What roles do a gaffer and best boy play in movie making?

Chief electrician, and chief electrician's assistant. The gaffer works with the director of photography and is responsible for everything to do with bringing electricity and lighting to the set. Many people work and assist on a movie set, but the "head" assistant to the gaffer is the best boy—whether or not it's a boy!

THIS IS EASY!

NO PROBLEM.

EASY AS PIE!

NO BIG DEAL.

OH-OH!

Y//////IKES!

?.

MAKE MY DAY!

coaster?

There are two—and they are both located in Japan. The Steel Dragon 2000 is over 1.5 miles long. The longest running coaster—at over 1.5 miles long in length—is Daidarasaurus of Expoland in Osaka.

135

How does a gasoline engine work?

A gasoline engine creates the force of energy that gets a vehicle going. *Combustion* is the key—a quick explosion that creates heat. This heat creates energy. In a car engine, a mixture of air and gasoline is lit by a spark in a *cylinder* containing a *piston*. (Think of a can with a disk-shaped plunger that fits exactly inside.) The heat from this little explosion makes the air expand and forces down the piston. The piston turns the *crankshaft*, a rod that is linked to the wheels. The wheels turn and off you go!

SPARK PLUG

CYLINDER

PISTON

CRANKSHAFT

BEEP-BEEP-BEEP

How can penguins tell each other apart?

It's all beak speak. When thousands of look-alike penguins gather in the same place each year for mating, the males attract females by *calling*. Couples "sing" together to learn each other's unique voice. Next year, when they return, many penguins find their long-lost mates from the year before. Scientists believe they can recognize each other's voice.

HI, JOE! HI, STACY! HI, JUDY! HI, TONY! HI, NINA! HI, MAX! HI, CHARYL! HI, BARNEY! I'M FRED! HI, MARIA! HI, MANNY!

Who invented BASKETBALL?

I DID!

A Canadian, Dr. James Naismith. In 1891, as an instructor at the International YMCA Training School in Massachusetts, the idea struck him. It was December and too cold to play outdoor sports. The game he created had nine players to a team, and the "hoops" were wooden peach baskets. Four years later basketball was played everywhere in the country. Now it's played practically everywhere in the world.

WHY DO I YAWN WHEN I GET SLEEPY?

To keep yourself up! A yawn is a slow, deep breath that brings more oxygen to the brain. It's a little like splashing cold water on your face. The oxygen gives your brain cells a little wake-up call.

WHAT'S THE HOTTEST SPICE IN THE WORLD?

It's a type of chile—the Red "Savina" habanero. And it's *hot, hot, hot*! The tiniest bit can be tasted in over 700 pounds of mild sauce. Can I have a barrel of icewater with that, please?

How can an airplane be made invisible?

It can't really . . . but it can be made to seem invisible. By using special lights on the outside of the plane, along with a special radar-absorbing surface and quiet engines, an aircraft can seem to disappear. During the day the panels of lights are used to make the plane appear the same brightness as the sky it flies in, which makes it impossible to see while it's flying. The radar-absorbent material on the outside of the airplane makes it impossible for radar to detect its presence. Combine these two factors with a very quiet engine and you'll never know it's there!

I'LL PUT THE TV ROOM HERE!

LODGE PLANS

Why do beavers build dams?

They're building a home. The amazing beaver "lodge" is a marvel of animal architecture. Beavers begin by cutting down trees with their sharp front teeth and powerful jaws. They use the tree trunks to build a watertight dam in a pond or lake. The dam is used to decrease the water level and to widen their living space. Then they build a room with rocks and twigs plastered together with mud. There's even a hole in the floor leading to the pond. Inside, beavers sleep and raise families.

WHERE IS TORNADO ALLEY?

What will cars be like in the future?

Energy efficient and independent. It's likely cars will be powered by rechargeable batteries, or use engines that run on renewable fuels such as water or carbon dioxide. It's also possible cars will drive themselves! These autonomous vehicles would navigate highways, traffic, and parking lots, and still maintain safe speeds and distances from other cars. And to improve fuel efficiency and allow hands-free driving, it's possible cars could somehow be hitched together in long lines. These "trains" of cars would conserve energy while being pulled along by the "engine" car in front.

If your skin is always renewing itself, how can you have a scar for life?

Your skin is like a rug woven of many fibers. If a cut isn't too wide, skin cells reweave the rug just like new. But if the cut edges are far apart, skin cells can't bridge the gap. Fibroblasts, cells that make bigger, tougher strands of skin, fill the space. This becomes a permanent scar.

In the plain states between the Rocky Mountains and the Appalachian Mountains. It's the area of the U.S. that produces the most tornadoes. The U.S. has about 1,000 tornadoes each year. Most of these occur in the central and southern plain states—Tornado Alley. More tornadoes strike Tornado Alley than any place else in the world. The world's deadliest tornado—the Tri State Tornado of March 18, 1925—cut a path 219 miles long across Missouri, Illinois, and Indiana. It killed 695 people, injured 1,980, and left 11,000 homeless.

I'LL TRY A COMIC STRIP NEXT!

SHOE STORE

WELCOME!

WHAT WERE THE FIRST KNOWN PAINTINGS?

The masterpieces of prehistoric people. On cave walls in France and Spain you can see paintings that were created between about 30,000 to 10,000 B.C. Early artists used natural substances from the earth for paint, and animal hair to make brushes. Mostly, they depicted the wild animals around them. The paintings have survived all these thousands of years, but some of them have only recently been discovered.

HOW MANY LEGS DOES A CENTIPEDE HAVE?

Most people think that a centipede has 100 legs, because the prefix "centi" means hundred. However, the largest centipedes, found in tropical climates, can be a foot long with as many as 340 legs! The average centipede may have only 70 legs and be about an inch long.

WHAT HAPPENS WHEN LIGHT IS REFLECTED THROUGH A PRISM?

It becomes a rainbow. Light is made up of tiny energy particles traveling in waves of different lengths. A prism—a clear geometric shape like a solid glass triangle—bends light and separates it into the colors of the rainbow. Red light bends the least and violet light bends the most. Droplets of water are the prisms that bend sunlight to create a rainbow in the sky.

When were plays first performed?

The earliest known plays were performed in Athens, Greece, around the sixth century B.C. They were part of a spring festival honoring the Greek god Dionysus.

Plays were also performed in ancient Egypt more than 5,000 years ago.

I FORGOT THE WORDS!

Who invented **VIDEO GAMES?**

ZAP!

POW!

In 1958, Willy Higinbotham invented the first video game. He created a "tennis game" that played on a five-inch screen. Each player held a small box with a knob and button on it. However, the first popular video game was developed by Nolan Bushnell in the 1970s. It was a screen version of Ping-Pong called "Pong." Most of today's video games are played on a computer and are much more challenging!

HOW CAN WATER CREATE ELECTRICITY?

The force of water falling over a dam can power machines that make electricity. Here's how it works. Water falls from a great height on to the paddles of a turbine—think of a pinwheel spinning when you blow on it. These giant metal turbines whirl up to 750 revolutions per minute. They provide the mechanical energy that rotates the magnet in an electrical generator. The generator uses magnets and copper wire to create electrical energy. This electricity travels through wires to the lightbulb in your lamp.

WOW! COOL!!

Are all snakes POISONOUS?

No. Snakes have a bad reputation because of the few poisonous ones. Of the 2,700 snake species, only about 400 are poisonous. Fewer than 50 kinds are dangerous to people. Most snakes will avoid people if at all possible. And most people will avoid snakes! The anaconda, weighing more than 500 pounds, is not poisonous but can squeeze the life out of a crocodile.

YOU RATTLE ME!

RATTLE!

LET ME GIVE YOU A HUG!

WHY DO BABY TEETH FALL OUT?

They need to be replaced by bigger, stronger adult teeth. As you get bigger, your mouth grows. When an adult tooth is ready to come in, it releases a chemical that dissolves the roots of the baby tooth it will replace. Without roots, the tooth is no longer anchored to the jawbone. It loosens and falls out—or gets pulled out! Now there is plenty of room for the larger, adult teeth!

How did the tooth fairy legend start?

Dr. Rosemary Wells, who researched the tooth fairy for more than 20 years, said that losing baby teeth has been important in all cultures, even ancient ones. It's a symbol of "leaving babyhood and entering childhood." Some countries have invented magical animals instead of a fairy. The United States is the only country with a tooth fairy who exchanges money for teeth! Dr. Wells opened a Tooth Fairy Museum in Illinois with all kinds of objects, even a singing tooth fairy toothbrush.

WHO WAS THE FIRST WOMAN IN SPACE?

I'M VALENTINA TERESHKOVA.

I'M SALLY RIDE

In June of 1963, Valentina Tereshkova of the former Soviet Union became the first woman in space. She spent 71 hours aboard Vostok 6. Sally Ride was the first American woman in space. An astrophysicist from California, Sally made her historic journey in 1983.

Why does poison ivy make people itch?

There's no poison in poison ivy, just an oil on the leaf that really clings to the skin. Your skin cells may detect this oil as an enemy. The cells rush to your defense, releasing chemicals that cause your skin to redden and blister, and ooze and itch, while they fight off the invader.

How did the black widow spider get its name?

By her nasty reputation. The black widow is a female spider that often eats the male she mates with! So when she kills her "husband," she becomes a "widow"— and a wicked one at that. Her venom is 15 times stronger than a rattlesnake's!

HOW DOES HYPNOTISM WORK?

Basically, your mind works on two levels. The one you are aware of is your thinking, *conscious* mind. The one you aren't aware of is your *subconscious* mind, which stores up memories, dreams, and hidden feelings. A hypnotist guides you to your subconscious mind by helping you become totally relaxed. Most techniques direct you to focus your thoughts on one thing. When you're hypnotized you are not asleep. You can be aware of everything going on around you, but you stay focused. It's a type of concentration similar to daydreaming in class. You get so caught up in your own mind that you don't hear the sounds of your teacher or classmates. Sometimes this state is called a trance.

WHY DOES JUMBO MEAN BIG?

Jumbo was an elephant who got his name from one of the most famous showmen who ever lived, P.T. Barnum (1810-1891), founder of the Barnum & Bailey Circus. Barnum was a man who knew how to capture an audience's attention. His elephant was big—11 feet tall and 6½ tons—and his catchy name made him so famous that "jumbo" came to mean huge, gigantic, enormous, or just plain large. We can thank Jumbo, who died in 1885, for a very modern phrase—the jumbo jet.

WHAT IS THE WORLD'S TALLEST STATUE?

A 394-foot statue of Buddha in Tokyo, Japan. Buddha, who lived from about 563 to 483 B.C., founded Buddhism, one of the great Asian religions. The bronze statue that honors him is 115 feet wide, and as tall as a 40-story skyscraper. The statue took seven years to build, and was finally completed in 1995.

How big can a lizard get?

That depends on the lizard's species. The smallest lizard, the dwarf gecko, is only about an inch long at its largest. The largest lizard species is the monitor lizard. There are about 30 kinds of monitors. The Nile monitor lizard, which can grow up to 7 feet long, is only medium-sized, as monitors go. The largest, the Komodo dragon, grows up to 10 feet long! Monitor lizards like warm weather—all 30 types live in tropical or subtropical areas.

KISS ME!

WHO INVENTED CHOCOLATE CHIP COOKIES?

Around 1930, while making cookies at the Toll House Inn in Whitman, Massachusetts, Ruth Wakefield found herself without baker's chocolate for her "butter drop do cookies," so she substituted a chocolate bar and cut it into bits. But the chocolate didn't completely melt and, thus, the chocolate chip cookie was born!

YUM!

YUM!

COOKIE!

ANY AGE LIKES THEM!

GO FOR IT!

Is there anything smaller than an atom?

Yes—the particles that make up an atom. Everything is made of atoms, including you and the chair you're sitting on. But they're so small—maybe a millionth of an inch—that they can be seen only with special microscopes. But an atom is made up of still smaller particles. At its center is a nucleus, which is 10,000 times smaller than the rest of the atom. And the nucleus is surrounded by electrons, which are even smaller!

WHAT MAKES MY STOMACH GROWL?

It's telling you it wants food to digest! Digestion happens automatically. When your stomach is empty its muscles still contract, as if it's looking for food. The walls squeeze together, creating the noises you hear. Digestive juices and acids roll around—rumbling, grumbling, and growling.

What is sleepwalking?

Walking in your sleep, without any idea that you're moving. Sleepwalkers commonly perform actions such as looking for lost objects or trying to solve other problems. But we don't know too much more than that. You might think that sleepwalking and dreaming go together, but they don't. Experiments show that sleepwalking occurs during very deep sleep. Dreaming occurs during light sleep.

DADDY!

SONNY!

WHO WAS THE ORIGINAL FRANKENSTEIN?

A man, not a monster. Dr. Frankenstein is the main character in a novel, written in 1818 by Mary Wollstonecraft Shelley. In the story, Dr. Frankenstein uses parts of dead bodies to make a creature who is very close to being human. This "monster" looks like a large, ugly man with greenish skin. After a zap with electricity, this strange fellow comes to life—and scares everyone to death. The name "Frankenstein" really belonged to his creator, but it stuck to the monster.

I THINK I SEE A PROTOZOAN!

I THINK I SEE A BLUE WHALE!

What is the smallest living creature in the world? The BIGGEST?

Protozoans, which can be found in most waters of the world, are the smallest. These microscopic members of the animal family are so tiny that 10,000 of them barely fill up an inch of space. Even so, their simple bodies have most of the same functions that ours do. On the other side of the scale is the blue whale, the largest animal that has ever lived on Earth. It can grow to 110 feet and weigh as much as 300,000 pounds.

How do meteorologists predict the weather?

IT'S A NICE DAY!

They start with the world and then concentrate on your neighborhood.

First, they look at the big picture. Thousands of weather stations around the world measure temperature, humidity, air pressure, and wind direction. Weather baloons and satellites also provide information.

Next, computer programs take all this information and predict how world weather conditions are likely to move and change.

Finally, meteorologists consider all these facts and make a good guess about what will happen where you live.

What is D-Day?

D-Day is the code name for the first day of a planned military attack. But World War II gave the name special meaning. During that war, Germany held France. But on D-Day, June 6, 1944, American, British, and other Allied soldiers attacked the Germans on the beaches of Normandy in France. That day was the beginning of the end for Germany, which surrendered less than a year later.

WE'VE LANDED ON OMAHA BEACH!

Why do eyes sometimes look **RED** in photos?

When a camera flash is pointed directly into your eyes, the light travels through your pupils. The camera actually takes a picture of the insides of your eyes. There are so many blood vessels in your eyes that the camera sees red.

What happens when water FREEZES?

Ice happens. Temperature affects the way molecules, the microscopic "building blocks" of a substance, bind together. At room temperature, water molecules are loosely connected. That's why water flows. But as the temperature drops to 32°F, water molecules slowly bind together until ice is formed.

HARD WATER!

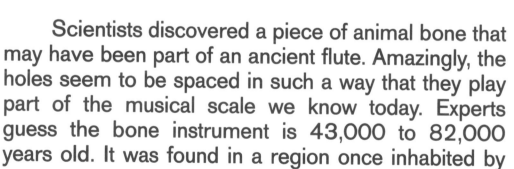

What was the world's first instrument?

Scientists discovered a piece of animal bone that may have been part of an ancient flute. Amazingly, the holes seem to be spaced in such a way that they play part of the musical scale we know today. Experts guess the bone instrument is 43,000 to 82,000 years old. It was found in a region once inhabited by the Neanderthals, an early human species. So it seems that *do*, *re*, *mi* has been around for a long, long time.

LET'S SIGN HIM UP FOR OUR ROCK BAND!

WHY DO MY EARS POP IN AN AIRPLANE?

CAPTAIN, I JUST HEARD A POP!

It's in the air. Your eardrum is in its normal position when the air pressure is the same inside and outside your ear. When an airplane goes up or down, the air pressure outside the plane changes. The pilot must adjust the pressure inside the plane. This quick change in air pressure may cause a bulge in your eardrum. When the air pressure becomes equal again, your eardrum "pops" back into place.

How many people have lived in the world since humans came to exist?

About fifty billion is the best guess, and the number is increasing. Every minute, approximately 160 babies are born around the world.

Where did bullfighting begin?

Even though bullfighting was known 4,000 years ago on the Greek island of Crete, Spain is the name to know when it comes to bulls and fighting. The Moors, Arabs who once ruled Spain, began the sport there in the 11th century. Today bullfighting is still popular in Spain, Portugal, Mexico, and parts of South America.

THAT'S A LOT OF BULL!

151

Who was Genghis Khan?

A man with a plan to conquer the whole world. Genghis Khan (1167-1227), originally named Temüjin, was a Mongolian leader who came to power at only 13 years of age. The young ruler soon became known as Genghis Khan—"precious warrior." He united the Mongol tribes into a fierce fighting force. They invaded what is now China, Russia, Iran, and northwest India, creating one of the greatest empires of all time. Upon Genghis Khan's death, the Mongol Empire was divided among his three sons and gradually dissolved.

Who invented gunpowder?

The Chinese. It was not meant for guns at first, but for fireworks. It was invented around 1000 A.D. and was probably a result of experiments attempting to turn chemicals and other substances into gold. Later, the Chinese used the explosive on the tips of arrows for rocket-like weapons. By the 1200s, gun powder was used by Europeans as well.

Why do monkeys and apes groom each other?

Why do humans shake hands or give hugs? Touching is a form of communication. A social act, grooming helps to keep a group of monkeys together. Grooming is also symbolic of a monkey's social status. A monkey grooms those with a higher social position and is groomed by those of lower rank. Above all, grooming keeps apes and monkeys clean!

What are geodes?

Round hollow rocks lined on the inside with fascinating, and sometimes beautiful, crystal formations. The most common type of geode forms from gas bubbles that get stuck inside a certain type of lava flow. Over time, the lava hardens and the bubbles transform into cavities surrounded by rock exteriors. Sometimes, while the lava is still hardening, hot water filters into the cavity. Other times, over the course of millions of years, mineralized ground water seeps in. But once the water is inside, crystals begin to grow—usually quartz. The exciting thing about geodes is you never know what they're like inside until you break them open!

What would happen if there were no more plants in the world?

Not much could happen. Plants are a necessary link in the cycle of nature that connects all living things. *Photosynthesis*, the process by which plants use sunlight to make their own food, supplies us with the oxygen we breathe. Plants are a source of food and shelter for many animals. Plants also keep the soil from blowing away in the wind. There would be no world as we know it without plants.

Do stars last forever?

No. Stars are mostly made up of hydrogen gas, which constantly burns. That's why stars shine. Eventually, they burn themselves up and explode, or simply burn out. How long that takes depends on the star. Giant stars, bigger than our sun, actually burn out quicker than smaller stars. Scientists believe our sun has been burning for five billion years—and it has five billion more to go. That's a long time, but it's not forever.

What animal is responsible for the most human deaths worldwide?

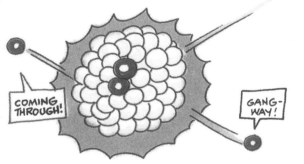

The mosquito. It may be tiny, but it can carry potentially deadly viruses. Malaria, which is transmitted by mosquitoes, infects 3 million people and is responsible for a million deaths—every year. Malaria is most dangerous in southern Africa due to the climate and lack of resources for fighting the disease. Also, the particular types of mosquito and form of the virus that inhabit that region are the most deadly.

HOW DOES SOMETHING BECOME RADIOACTIVE?

HERE I COME!

COMING THROUGH!

GANG-WAY!

Atoms are the tiny "building blocks" of all substances. Atoms contain energy. Over time, the *nucleus*, or center, of every atom decays. When this happens, parts of the atom shoot out in high-energy rays. This is called nuclear radiation, or radioactivity. When something is radioactive it becomes electrically charged. Most radioactive rays are too weak to harm us, but strong rays can be dangerous. Radioactivity is helpful for scientists who do medical research or study the Earth.

How many African Americans served in the Civil War?

Approximately 180,000—or 10 percent of the entire Union forces. Many wanted to join the Union army earlier but were prevented by old laws. It was President Lincoln's Emancipation Proclamation in 1862 that finally allowed African Americans to enlist. They served bravely and tirelessly, despite the prejudice and unequal treatment they received even while fighting and risking all for their country.

154

How much BLOOD is in my body?

HE USED HIS NOODLE!

DID SOMEBODY SAY *BLOOD*?

I'D RATHER HAVE PASTA!

A grown-up has about five quarts of blood in his or her body. That means you probably have about three or four quarts of blood in your body. There are four quarts in a gallon. To get an idea of how much that is, think of one big container of milk—or about 16 glasses full!

WHO CREATED SPAGHETTI?

The legend says that Italian explorer Marco Polo brought spaghetti back from China in 1292. However, carvings in a 5,000-year-old tomb near Rome show all the tools needed to make pasta. So who did it first—China or Italy? We may never know, but there is general agreement that Naples, Italy, is the birthplace of spaghetti as we know it today.

Naples

China

155

WHO INVENTED THE JIGSAW PUZZLE?

An Englishman who wanted to teach a geography lesson. In 1767, John Spilsbury carved a wooden map of England and divided it into counties. Each county was one piece. They fit around each other according to their location. The carboard jigsaw puzzles we know today were developed in the 20th century.

I'M FAMOUS!

What is PLASTIC made of?

STRING

HAMMER

DAMPER

How does a PIANO make sound when you press a key?

Each of a piano's 88 keys is attached to at least one steel wire string. Each string has a "hammer" that strikes it. Pressing a key causes the hammer to strike its string. When the string is struck, it vibrates and makes the sound you think of as a "note." All together, there are nearly 4,000 parts in the action of one piano. And with only ten fingers, you can make all this action happen.

KEY

WE GO THROUGH ALL THIS JUST TO MAKE A SOUND... NOW DON'T FORGET TO PRACTICE!

Where is the Great Barrier Reef?

It stretches along the northeast coast of Australia—for 1,250 miles! A reef is a ridge in the ocean close to the surface of the water. The Great Barrier Reef, made up of the remains of tiny sea creatures, is a chain of more than 2,500 reefs. Billions and billions of coral skeletons have been piling up for nearly 15 million years to form this reef, the largest in the world.

Mixed-up oil molecules. Scientists discovered plastic by rearranging some of the molecules in oil. The process is called *polymerization*. Many *synthetic* (human-made) substances are created this way, including different kinds of plastic. The first useful plastic was celluloid, invented in 1870 by John Hyatt. It was used to make billiard balls. Maybe he liked to shoot pool!

WHAT IS SPELUNKING?

It's a hobby for people who like to take the plunge—into caves. "Spelunking" comes from the word *speleology*, which is the scientific study of caves. Spelunkers, unlike speleologists, are people who explore caves just for fun. The bravest spelunkers have inched their way down as deep as 3,000 feet.

I'M SAM THE SPELUNKER.

WHICH WAY?

Who was AMELIA EARHART?

A daring pilot with a mysterious death. Earhart (1897–1937) was the first woman to fly solo across the Atlantic Ocean—but that's not all. She also made the first solo flight from Hawaii to the United States mainland, and she was also the first woman to fly nonstop across the United States. But she never completed her flight around the world. During that voyage in 1937, Earhart's plane disappeared over the Pacific Ocean—and not a trace was ever found.

HOW DOES A FAX MACHINE KNOW WHAT TO PRINT?

Electricity is used by the fax machine to "see" what it's printing. Fax is short for facsimile, which means a copy. When you send a fax, you send a copy of words or pictures to a fax machine at another location. A scanner in the fax machine "reads" the images by coding the dark areas in electrical signals. The signals travel over telephone wires. Finally, the printer in the receiving machine prints out the dark pattern in tiny dots, just the way your machine sent them.

Why is it easier to balance on my bicycle when it's moving than when it's standing still?

A spinning wheel will stay upright on its own. This motion is called *precession*. You've seen it in a spinning top. The faster it spins, the longer the top stays up. As the spinning slows down, the top begins to wobble. The same goes for a bicycle wheel. The faster it spins, the more likely it is to stay up—and so are you!

THAT'S GREAT... BUT, I'M LOST!

How does a thermometer work?

Heat and the metal mercury work together in a glass thermometer. A thermometer is a thin tube of glass with a hollow bulb at one end. The bulb is filled with mercury. When the mercury is heated, it expands and moves up the tube. The distance it moves is measured in degrees.

IT'S HOT TODAY!

NORTH POLE

What is the midnight sun?

When the sun can be seen in the sky continuously for 24 hours or more. This is also known as "white nights." Midnight sun occurs in the Arctic and Antarctic during summer months. Summer begins about June 22 in the Arctic; about December 22 in the Antarctic. "Land of the Midnight Sun" is a nickname for any country—such as Finland, Norway, or Sweden—where the midnight sun can be seen.

HOW LARGE WAS THE LARGEST CAKE EVER BAKED?

It was 130,000 pounds. It was 102 feet long, 52 feet wide, and 20 inches high. The icing alone weighed almost 40,000 pounds. The cake was baked to celebrate the 100th birthday of Las Vegas, a city that likes to have big parties!

A MASTERPIECE

WOW!

LOOKS DELICIOUS.

ARF! (YUM!)

Why do we itch? Does scratching STOP an itch?

Itching and scratching seem simple, but they're mysterious. Scientists don't know exactly how to explain itching. We do know that certain sensations cause us to itch. For example, if an ant marched across your foot, it would itch. To stop the itching you would scratch. Scratching is a much more power-ful sensation, so the itch seems to go away.

What do Mars and Venus look like?

MARS — I'M COLD.
EARTH — I'M JUST RIGHT.
THE MOON — I'M HOT AND COLD!
VENUS — I'M HOT!

Mars is named for the Roman god of war because it looks blood red. When space scientists took a closer look, they realized that the color is caused by rusted iron in the soil. The surface of Mars is covered by rocks and mountains. *Olympus Mons*, 16 miles high, is the tallest mountain in our solar system.

The rocky surface of Venus has large craters and high mountains. But the surface is difficult to see because the planet is surrounded by thick clouds. The clouds reflect and absorb sun-light, making Venus the hottest planet—over 800°F—and one of the brightest in our solar system.

What are CRYSTALS

made of?

Minerals are the basic elements of crystals. Crystals form when molten minerals, or minerals dissolved in heated liquid, cool. Each type of mineral forms crystals with particular shapes. For example, the mineral *galena*, the main source of lead, forms four-sided cubic crystals. Even though crystals are nonliving substances, they can "grow," or increase, by forming the same link over and over. This process is called *crystallization*.

Who invented LANGUAGE?

No one knows for sure because there are certainly no written records of how words developed! Scholars think written language may have begun around 3000 B.C., because the Sumerians of the Middle East started writing around that time. This early form of writing, called *cuneiform* (kyu-NEE-uh-form), used symbols for whole words. The alphabet was invented in the Middle East around 1500 B.C. by the Phoenicians.

Why doesn't it hurt a kitten when its mother picks it up by the scruff of its neck?

PUT ME DOWN MOM!

Kittens have plenty of loose skin around their neck, so the mother can get a good grip without pulling too hard. She hangs on to the skin but is careful not to bite. The kitten also cooperates by staying still. That way it's an easy, painless ride.

SOB! I'M NOT REAL! SOB!

DO VAMPIRES REALLY EXIST?

Of course not! Vampires were made up by good storytellers. Still, the idea of a body rising from the grave to suck your blood is so horrible, some people are scared into believing vampires exist. According to legend, sleeping with garlic around your neck or putting salt on your windowsill ought to keep vampires away.

How does a cell phone work?

With radio signals and transmitters. "Cells" refers to the 10-square-mile units that cell phone companies divide cities and towns into. Each unit, or cell, has its own cell tower and base station. Signals from a cell phone transmit to the nearest cell tower, and then to the phone of the person you're calling. If you use a cell phone in a moving vehicle—or walk a long distance—your phone's signal gets passed from one transmitter to the next, or from cell to cell.

What is the difference between honeybees and wasps?

IF I STING YOU . . . I'M HISTORY !!

I HATE THE WINTER!

They belong to the same family, *Apoidea*, but there are many differences. Honeybees live in hives. Some wasps build a nest out of "paper," which they make by chewing on wood and passing it through their bodies. Another difference is that honeybees collect the sweet nectar from flowers to make honey. Wasps make a meal of other insects. Also, if a honeybee stings, it loses its stinger and dies. Not the wasp: It stings and lives to sting again. One more difference: Honeybees live through the winter. Wasps, alas, do not.

Where is the longest river in the world? Where is the deepest lake?

NILE RIVER

I LIVE HERE.

The world's longest river is the Nile, which runs through the countries of Egypt and Sudan, in northeastern Africa. It is about 4,160 miles long.

Siberia, a region in Russia, is home to Lake Baikal, the world's deepest lake. Its lowest point plunges more than a mile below the surface—5,315 feet.

HOW DOES A GLACIER FORM?

I'M IN NO RUSH!

Glaciers form at high elevations when more snow falls than melts, causing it to build up. The pressure of all that snow causes glacial ice to form. The ice becomes so heavy that the glaciers begins to move. Most glaciers travel slowly—only about a foot a day. A glacier can grow to more than half a mile thick, and can be the size of a small island or continent! In fact, 98% of the continent of Antarctica is covered by a glacier.

How does a digital camera work?

EVERYONE THAT'S LOOKING AT THIS PAGE SMILE!

In the blink of an eye. When you snap a photo, you focus the light that bounces off an image using the lens of your camera. A digital camera stores the image as a collection of pixels using a tiny microprocessor it has inside. There's no film in a digital camera, but the information stored in the microchip can be downloaded to a computer, which can then print out pictures or display them on screen.

What is the ozone layer?

It's part of Earth's atmosphere. As you go up from the ground, the gases that make up the atmosphere change. These "layers" of gas have different names. The ozone layer is about 12 to 30 miles above Earth's surface. Ozone is a form of oxygen that absorbs much of the sun's ultraviolet radiation and prevents it from reaching the ground. If this radiation did reach ground level, it would be harmful to most forms of life.

163

How does water get to my sink?

It starts in a natural source like a lake, river, or reservoir. The water is pumped through pipes into large tanks. Fish, plants, and trash are screened out. Chemicals like chlorine are added to kill any bacteria or dangerous substances. If you live in a city, the water is then pumped into cast iron pipes called mains. The mains run beneath the streets and carry water to every hydrant, house, and building. The pumping station sends the water to every faucet. If you live in a rural area, water is pumped from a well right into your house. Turn it on!

TIME TO DRY OFF!

WHAT IS A BRUISE?

I WALKED INTO A DOOR KNOB!

A bruise is a bunch of broken blood vessels beneath the skin. When they break, blood oozes out into the tissues around the spot. The tissues turn a purplish color. As the bruise heals, it changes into a rainbow of colors—first blue, then green, and finally yellow before it disappears. This happens as the blood is absorbed into the body again.

THAT'S NOT A GOOD IDEA!

Why do people eat turkey on Thanksgiving?

It has become a tradition. The first Thanksgiving in the New World was a celebration by the Pilgrims in 1621. It was an effort to thank the Native Americans who had helped the Pilgrims survive their first year. Our only real clue that they ate turkey is in a letter written by one of the men. It said the governor sent four men "fowling" for the feast. A turkey is a fowl—a bird that people eat—and there were plenty of wild turkeys roaming the woods in Massachusetts. Also, since Massasoit, the Indian chief, brought 90 people for dinner, fat turkeys would have been very useful. By the early 1800s turkey became the Thanksgiving bird of America.

LET'S CHANGE IT TO HOT DOGS!

What is the Nobel Prize?

Annual awards given to people around the world who make "contributions to the good of humanity." Alfred Bernhard Nobel (1833–1896) was a Swedish chemist who invented dynamite and became extremely rich. He never got over the destruction his invention caused. Before he died, Nobel established a fund for prizes in physics, chemistry, medicine, literature, economics, and peace.

WHAT ANIMAL HAS TEETH ALL OVER ITS BODY?

THE LAST TIME I SAW A DENTIST I ATE HIM!

Sharks— as if the teeth in their mouth aren't enough! A shark doesn't have scales on its body like other fish. Most sharks have *denticles* instead. A shark's body is covered with these small, razor-sharp, toothlike constructions. Denticles overlap like scales, but if you rubbed up against them, they would rip right through your skin!

What happened during the GOLD RUSH?

During the 1800s in North America there were several gold discoveries. As soon as someone discovered gold, people "rushed" to the spot hoping to get rich. California, Colorado, and Alaska are the most famous gold-digging spots. In 1848, gold was found near a small town called San Francisco. A year later, 25,000 people lived there. In just one more year, there were so many miners in the territory that California had enough people to become a state.

I'M RICH! I'M RICH!!

GET A SHAVE!

Where is the world's BIGGEST gingerbread house?

It was in Minnesota, in one of the largest indoor shopping malls. In November 2006, a team of people spent 1,700 hours putting together 14,250 pounds of gingerbread and 4,750 pounds of frosting. Their masterpice was as tall as a five-story house—60 feet high—until everyone ate it!

I'M GOOD ENOUGH TO EAT!

I'LL EAT THE TV ROOM!

I WANT THE KITCHEN!

YUM!

I'LL TAKE THE FRONT DOOR!

YUM... THE GUEST ROOM!

I UNDERSTAND THAT THE CHIMNEY IS DELICIOUS!

How does an egg hatch?

It's all in the tooth—the egg tooth. Both baby birds and reptiles chip their way out of a shell with a small, sharp tooth. A bird's egg tooth grows on its beak. A snake's is on its upper jaw. After the work of hatching is done, the egg tooth falls away.

I'M BUSTING OUT OF HERE!

Who built the GIGANTIC statues on Easter Island and why?

I DON'T KNOW!

BEATS ME!

It remains a mystery, but most experts believe it was the Polynesians who lived on Easter Island 2,000 years ago. Whoever built the statues used only stone tools. Most of the square-shaped human figures weigh about 20 tons, but the biggest weighs around 50 tons and stands 69 feet tall. Hundreds of the enormous statues, built on temple platforms, face the empty landscape. Scholars believe they are images of chiefs or spiritual leaders, but we may never know their true story.

WHY IS IT HOTTER NEAR THE EQUATOR?

The equator is the great imaginary line that circles Earth halfway between the North and South Poles. It's this location that makes the equator such a hot spot. Because the Earth is curved, the most direct sunlight rays strike at the equator. The least direct sunlight hits the poles. But in Ecuador, a country on the equator, the city of Quito has a very high elevation. The altitude cools the temperature down to an average of about 58°F.

EQUATOR

What is the world's most popular spectator sport?

OUCH!

Soccer, which has been popular for quite a while. A ball made of animal skins may have been kicked around in ancient China. But other countries want to take credit for soccer, including Japan, Mexico, and Greece. Native Americans played a game in the 1600s called *pasuckuakohowog*, which means "they gather to play ball with the foot." The English finally set down regular rules for the game in 1863. Today, soccer is played in 140 nations and the whole world watches it!

What animal has eyes at the end of its arms, and feet under its arms?

I DON'T.

The starfish. The "sea star" (its real name) is not necessarily a star and not a fish at all. It's a creature that lives in the ocean and takes several shapes. The most common is the five-pointed star—five "arms" with a body in the center.

The sea star "sees" with a small colored eyespot at the tip of each arm. These eyespots sense light but can't form images. The feet are rows of slender tubes that extend from the body to the end of each arm. With a suction disk at each tip, the sea star crawls along the ocean floor.

WHY DO FLEAS LIVE ON CATS AND DOGS?

I'M MOVING!

Your pets are the fleas' dinner. Warm-blooded animals such as cats, dogs, squirrels, birds, and even humans are all on the flea menu. Blood is what fleas are after. Fleas can be controlled with certain kinds of chemicals called insecticides, as well as ordinary soap! Believe it or not, staying clean helps make your pet unfit for fleas to grow on. A flea collar coated with chemicals helps, too!

WHERE WAS THE WORLD'S BIGGEST FIREWORKS DISPLAY?

It was not the Fourth of July. The big bang was in Madeira Island, Portugal, on January 1, 2008, and welcomed in the new year. The flash and light included 67 thousand fireworks—an eight-minute display with over 8 thousand fireworks launched each minute! Held over the bay, the celebration marked the 500th birthday of the Portuguese city of Funchal.

How is a bridge made?

Very carefully! The idea behind all bridges is to build a structure that shifts its weight to places where it can be supported. There are four main types of bridges.

Beam bridge: A flat road goes across a short, shallow river. It's held up by a long line of straight piers (supports) placed in the river floor.

Arch bridge: The road is placed over one or more arches built over the river. The weight of the road creates pressure that shifts down each side of the bridge to the "feet" anchored in the earth.

Cantilever bridge: There are two sections, one on each side of the river. The balance between the two sides supports a road between them.

WE ALL HAVE TOLLS!

Suspension bridge: The road is hung from giant, thick steel cables. These anchored cables shift the road's weight to the ground. One of the best-known suspension bridges is the Golden Gate Bridge in San Francisco, California.

What is NASA?

The National Aeronautics and Space Administration. NASA is an organization in the United States that manages the development and operation of aircrafts in space. It all began in 1958 and has included everything from the first manned flight, to landing on the moon, to satellites that explore other planets, to space shuttles and space stations. Most NASA flights take off from the Kennedy Space Center in Cape Canaveral, Florida. NASA's "command center" is in Houston, Texas.

Who were the Maya?

People who spoke the Mayan language and whose civilization reached its greatest height from A.D. 200 to 800. The Maya lived in what are now areas of Belize, Guatemala, El Salvador, and Mexico. Many years before the Europeans, the Maya developed a calendar and used mathematics. They also created an advanced form of writing. Their pottery and sculpture are treasured today, and some of their magnificent temples are still standing. Six million Maya still speak the old languages and keep the ancient traditions alive.

WHAT IS SOLAR HEATING?

Sun power, which creates a great deal of heat. But it's difficult to capture the heat, store it, and use it when you need it. Solar heating is an effort to do just that. Special plates installed on the roof of a house absorb heat from the sun. Once absorbed, the heat is stored in water or rocks in a large container. A heating system circulates the heat throughout the house. Even experimental solar-powered cars have been built!

WARM ME UP!

DON'T WARM ME UP!

HOW BIG WAS THE WORLD'S BIGGEST SNOWMAN?

If you were on the top floor of a ten-story building and stuck your head out the window, you could be nose to nose with the world's biggest snowman. In Maine, in 1999, a group of people who probably like cold weather spent two weeks building "Angus." When they were done, Frosty the Snowman had a 113-foot-high big brother!

WHY DOES THE MOON LOOK LIKE SWISS CHEESE?

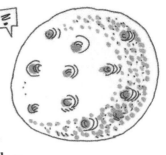

Swiss cheese has holes. The moon has craters, or pits, in the surface. Some of the craters are small, but others are huge—up to 155 miles across—and can be seen from Earth. Most of the craters were made during early periods of the solar system, when space was a traffic jam of rocks and metal flying off the planets as they formed. When these fragments crashed into the moon, the impact caused craters.

Why do babies cry?

To communicate. Babies can't say "I'm so hungry I could eat a horse" or "Get me out of this car seat." So they make the only noise they can—crying. If you're around a baby, you can tell the difference between crying that means hungry, angry, tired, or scared.

Where does the word "Eureka" come from?

Greece. Archimedes (287–212 B.C.) was a Greek mathematician and inventor. The story is that he had just stepped into one of the public baths when an idea came to him. He was so excited that he rushed home yelling "Eureka! Eureka!" (I have found it! I have found it!) So when you discover something you've been looking for, shout "Eureka!"

WHAT IS A MARSUPIAL?

Kangaroos are the most famous marsupials, but some others are opossums, koalas, and wombats. What makes them different from other animals is the "pouch" just below their stomach. The pouch is for carrying their offspring.

Marsupial babies do more of their growing outside the mother's body than inside. At birth, they are very underdeveloped and less than an inch long. These tiny creatures struggle up through their mother's fur and crawl into her pouch. Inside they find nipples for milk and a safe place to hide. A baby kangaroo stays there for five to ten months.

THAT'S MY MOM!

171

Who was Gandhi?

Mohandas Gandhi (1869-1948) guided India to independence from Britain. Called the *Mahatma*, meaning "great soul," Gandhi believed in nonviolence, courage, and truth. At times, he fasted to show belief in his cause. In 1948, one year after India was granted independence, conflicts broke out between Muslims and Hindus. Gandhi encouraged them to live peacefully, and was killed by a Hindu who disagreed with him.

I'M HUNGRY!

HOW DOES A CLAM EAT?

It opens its shell slightly to let dinner in. Tiny hairs filter food into a small mouth, then into the stomach. The food is digested there and absorbed into the intestines. Clams eat tiny water plants and sea animals called plankton. Although clams seem to be bloblike creatures, they have a digestive system, and even a heart and blood vessels.

HOW DOES MY VOICE WORK?

It's all in your vocal cords, a pair of muscles in your windpipe. When air from your lungs passes over your vocal cords, they vibrate. To make sounds, your vocal cords need to contract, or tighten, rather than relax. You control that. The more your vocal cords contract, the more high-pitched the sound.

Your mouth and tongue form these sounds into words.

Why does the word "LOVE" mean ZERO POINTS in tennis?

It certainly doesn't mean tennis players love to lose! The answer is hidden between two languages. Tennis began in France in the 1100s or 1200s. "Love" may have come from the French word *l'oeuf*, which was slang for zero. The English, who invented the modern version of tennis in the late 1800s, pronounced it "luff." Eventually, it became love.

WHO INVENTED PLAYING CARDS?

MY MUMMY TAUGHT ME HOW TO PLAY CARDS.

History has hidden the answer. People must have been too busy playing to stop and say, "Hey, who made up this game?" Most scholars believe that some form of cards began in India and developed in Egypt in the 12th and 13th centuries. By 1380, cards were known in Italy, Switzerland, France, and Spain. In 1452, playing cards were burned in bonfires as a reaction to gambling.

What is the Venus flytrap?

LUNCH TIME!

The Venus flytrap is one of 500 types of *carnivorous*, or meat-eating, plants. The plant eats mostly insects though, so don't worry. The two-sided leaves of the Venus are the "fly trap." Each is lined with toothlike spines. When an insect flies inside and touches the trigger hairs...SNAP! The two sides of the leaf clamp together. The insect is caught and slowly digested (it takes about 10 days). Finally, the leaf opens again. After two or three catches, the leaves die and are replaced by younger, snappier leaves.

173

WHAT IS A WINDMILL USED FOR?

Windmills use the force of the wind to produce power. Wind whips through the blades, which are attached to a shaft. The shaft, which runs down the tower, is connected to an underground pump or mechanical gears. Windmills are used for such tasks as milling grain, pumping water for farmland, pressing oil from seeds, and grinding different materials. Wind turbine generators use the power of the wind to generate electricity. They have huge, propellerlike blades.

What was the PONY EXPRESS?

Eighty mailmen on horseback. The pony express was a well organized mail-delivery system that operated between Missouri and California. In the 1860s, it took teamwork to get mail to its destination. Riders galloped at full speed, stopping at stations every ten miles or so to change horses. Each rider traveled up to 100 miles of the total route—1,966 miles. They hauled the mail in pouches, carrying two guns and a knife to protect themselves against bandits. The whole trip was made in about eight or nine days. One of the riders was 14-year-old William Cody, later known as Buffalo Bill.

How are fossils formed? Where are they found?

When an animal or plant dies, it decays over time. Sometimes, if conditions are right, the earth preserves traces of the animal or plant—for millions of years! Imagine an ancient reptile that died in mud. Its flesh would decay. The bones would slowly dissolve, but minerals might fill in the spaces, harden, and preserve the shape of the bones. That's called a *petrified* fossil. A *mold* fossil is created when an animal or plant dies and its shape forms an impression in the earth. Fossils are found all over the world in places where ancient rocks have been uncovered.

I WAS IN AN ACCIDENT.

DO INSECTS HAVE A HEART AND BLOOD?

Yes—tiny as they may be, insects have pretty complicated working parts. An insect's heart is a long tube that runs along the top of its body. It pumps blood, which brings digested food to the organs and takes away waste materials. The blood doesn't carry oxygen, so it isn't red like ours. It is light green, yellowish, or clear.

Why is a black cat considered unlucky?

I AM?!

If you fear a black cat crossing your path, blame it on witches. Witchcraft has been around since ancient times. At one time, people believed that each witch had an assistant, or personal demon, called a familiar. Familiars took the form of animals— and many were black cats.

THAT'S MY PET CAT,

Why does Saturn have rings around it?

The planet is surrounded by chunks of ice, plus some dust and metal materials. These particles orbit around Saturn like satellites. Also orbiting Saturn are small *moonlets*, celestial bodies with their own gravitational pull. Scientists believe that the pull of these moonlets keeps the particles together, forming the rings. The rings whirl around Saturn, shining with light coming from the sun.

NOT THAT KIND OF RING!

How are animals trained?

YUM! I DID GOOD!

Most animals learn by a method called *operant conditioning*. Basically, each time an animal performs a behavior the trainer has in mind, it receives a reward. The reward is called a *reinforcer* because it reinforces, or encourages, the behavior. Animals don't "think" as we do, but they can learn behaviors in this way. Gorillas, chimpanzees, and marine mammals are trained by this method.

Who was SACAJAWEA?

FOLLOW ME.

A Native American woman, of the Shoshone tribe, who made an important contribution to the exploration of America. In 1804, explorers Meriwether Lewis and William Clark set out from St. Louis to find a route to the west coast. Sacajawea went with them as a guide. Their journey would have been much harder without her. She saved them weeks of travel time because she knew the territory and the mountain passes. She found food when it was scarce by gathering wild plants. Lewis and Clark were so grateful, they named a river, a mountain peak, and a mountain pass in her honor.

Does a rain dance work?

If it did, we would have rain whenever our rivers run dry or when crops need water. Many ancient cultures believed that the important forces of nature, like the sun, the earth, and the rain, were gods. It was their way of explaining how the universe worked. To them, it made sense to pray to the god of rain if rain were needed. Many of the songs and dances in these rituals were very beautiful.

WHEN WERE FORKS INVENTED?

The first forks probably had two prongs and were used to hold meat over a fire. It wasn't until the 1500s in Italy that forks were used at the table, and then only by people who cared enough to keep their shirtsleeves out of their food. Still, forks weren't very common. If you think about it, most foods can be eaten without a fork—but it's hard to eat soup without a spoon!

WHAT'S THE OLDEST INSECT?

The cockroach! Those pesky pests have been around for 350 million years, and they look pretty much the same now as they did then. They have flat bodies, long legs, and range from about one-quarter inch to three inches long. What incredible survivors!

I'VE BEEN AROUND!

How *FAST* can a cheetah run?

Seventy miles an hour in 25-foot leaps. When it comes to short distances, the cheetah is the fastest land animal on earth. The cat's flexible spine is the secret to its speed. The spine curls and uncurls like elastic, springing the cheetah forward. Speedier than a sports car, the cat bursts from zero to 40 miles per hour in two seconds!

I GOT A TICKET FOR SPEEDING!

SPEEDING TICKET - 40 MPH IN A 20 MPH ZONE

WHY DO I GET THIRSTY?

ANCHOVY PIZZA MAKES ME THIRSTY!!

Your body is trying to tell you something. It's saying you don't have enough water in your bloodstream. Strangely, people who are dehydrated (seriously lacking water) tend to drink just what they need. Scientists think we must have a "water meter" in our bodies, but they haven't found it yet. Salty food also makes us thirsty because salt absorbs water. When you drink enough water to satisfy your body, your thirst is quenched!

IT'S A WHALE OF A PLACE!

NORTH POLE

WHAT'S THE DIFFERENCE BETWEEN THE ARCTIC AND THE ANTARCTIC?

The Arctic is home of the North Pole. The Arctic Circle, an imaginary line 1,630 miles below the Pole, marks the entire region—including the Arctic Ocean, many islands, and northern parts of Europe, Asia, and North America. It's very cold in the Arctic, but in some areas the snow disappears in the summer. The Arctic is home to polar bears, seals, whales, musk oxen, caribou, and birds.

The Antarctic is home of the South Pole. The region covers over five million square miles. At its greatest distance, the icy continent of Antarctica is 3,250 miles across. A few mosses and just two flowering plants manage to survive—along with a small, wingless fly. The Antarctic Ocean is home to fish, birds, seals, whales, and penguins.

SOUTH POLE

IT'S A WHALE OF A PLACE!

Who was Madame Curie?

The first person to be awarded two Nobel Prizes, and the only person to get one in two different fields. She and her husband, Pierre, discovered the radioactive element polonium (which they named after Poland, the country of her birth). Later, they discovered an even stronger radioactive element, radium. It was Madame Curie who discovered that radioactivity is a property of the atoms that make up an element. The Curies and Henri Becquerel shared the 1903 Nobel Prize in Physics. In 1911, Madame Curie received the Nobel Prize in Chemistry. Later, she devoted her life to working on the use of x-rays in medicine.

Where did the expression "GOING BANANAS" come from?

We say someone is "going bananas" when they're being silly or ridiculous. Monkeys can act pretty crazy, swinging from trees, whooping and calling—and they do love bananas. So, "going bananas" is the human version of all this monkey business.

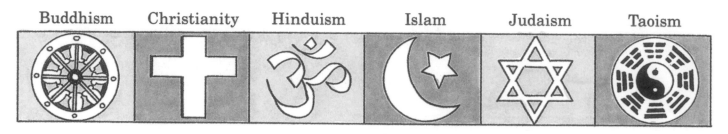

| Buddhism | Christianity | Hinduism | Islam | Judaism | Taoism |

How many religions are there in the world?

The religions that are most organized, and that have the most followers today, are Buddhism, Christianity, Hinduism, Islam, Judaism, and Taoism. That makes six, but there are many other religions practiced around the world.

What is the Parthenon?

A surviving building of the ancient world. The Parthenon is a temple in Athens, Greece, built in the fifth century B.C. to honor Athena, goddess of war, peace, and wisdom. It stands on a hill called the Acropolis, which overlooks the city. Many of the sculptures from the Parthenon are considered among the world's greatest works of art.

Who invented the YO-YO?

Yo-yos were known in ancient China and Greece, but the Philippines put the yo-yo on the modern map. In the 16th century, Filipinos used yo-yos to snare animal prey from trees. As you can imagine, Filipinos became very good yo-yo players! In 1920, American Donald F. Duncan saw a Filipino man yo-yoing. Soon after, Duncan went into the yo-yo business and made it the world's most famous toy. Since then, going "Around the World" has become a well-known maneuver. In 1992, a yo-yo went aboard the space shuttle Atlantis and traveled 3,321,007 miles—going around the world, for real, 127 times!

What is Dr. Seuss's REAL NAME?

Theodor Seuss Geisel (1904–1991)—better known as Dr. Seuss, the Pulitzer prize-winning author of 47 children's books. His work takes place in a silly make-believe world filled with truffula trees, ziffs and zuffs, and nerkles and nerds, but each book has something to say to adults and children about real life. "I like nonsense," Dr. Seuss said. "It wakes up the brain cells." Among his most famous books are *The Cat in the Hat*, *Green Eggs and Ham*, and *How the Grinch Stole Christmas*.

WHY DO WE BREATHE?

We breathe because every cell in the body needs oxygen from the air to stay alive. When air comes into the lungs, oxygen is passed into the bloodstream. The bloodstream carries oxygen to the cells. Along the way, blood picks up waste called carbon dioxide and returns it to the lungs, where it is breathed out. Breathing is automatic—we don't have to think about it. You take about 20,000 breaths a day, which could add up to over 600 million in your lifetime.

How is RUBBER made?

I'M A BIG SAP!

Natural rubber comes from the sap of certain trees, and synthetic rubber is made by people. Rubber trees are found mostly in tropical climates. To make the trees' sap into a useful product called *latex*, water is removed and chemicals are added. The latex is then rolled into rubber sheets. Synthetic rubber is made from coal, oil, and natural gas. Rubber is one of the most useful products in the world. It holds air and keeps out moisture. It's elastic and durable. Some of the rubber products we use are tires, boots, raincoats, balls, erasers, and, of course, rubber bands!

Who was the youngest ruler of a nation?

A two-year-old boy, Emperor Hsuan T'ung, the last emperor of China. He was born in 1906. Just six years later, a revolution swept the country and everything changed. Henry P'u-i, as the young emperor was known, was forced to leave China. He did return, but was put in jail. Finally, for the 10 years before he died in 1967, T'ung was allowed to work as a gardener at one of the colleges in Beijing, the capital of China. So, at the end of his life, the last emperor was ruled by others.

HOW FAST ARE THE FASTEST TRAINS?

The TGV (Train à Grande Vitesse) is a high-speed electric train system in France. The TGV is capable of incredible speeds—its record is 320 miles per hour—but even its regular cruising speed of 186 mph is *fast*.

The high-speed maglev (magnetic levitation) in Shanghai, China, is basically a train that floats on an electromagnetic cushion and zooms along a guideway at incredible speeds. Shanghai's new express can reach a top speed of 267mph in just under two minutes. That's *very fast!*

> I'M ALMOST FASTER THAN A SPEEDING BULLET!

Who was Aesop and why was he famous all over the world?

> DO YOU WANT TO RACE?

> SURE! HO-HUM.

> READY? SET? GO!!

Aesop was a Greek storyteller who lived from about 620 to 560 B.C. Since then, his fables have circled the world. Fables tell us about human behavior. In *The Tortoise and the Hare*, the two animals run a race. The speedy rabbit is so sure of winning that he takes his time and even naps. But the slow tortoise "keeps on trucking" and wins the race. Aesop's moral, or lesson, is that determination and steady work will get you where you want to go every time.

HOW DO TERMITES BUILD A MOUND?

Termites build big homes called "mounds" by cementing bits of soil together with their saliva. There are many different types of termites, but the big builders live in colonies that can have millions of members. Their mounds can be 20 to 30 feet high, filled with a maze of tunnels and chambers. Each colony has workers, soldiers, and a king and queen who live in a central chamber. The queen is enormous compared to the others. Her job is to lay thousands of eggs a day. Such termites are most common in warm regions in Africa, Australia, and South America.

IT'S A LOT OF WORK!

What is LEVITATION?

WOW!

Have you ever seen a magician float a person in the air? That's levitation. How is it done? It's the magician's secret, but you can be sure it's a trick. Some people, however, believe we can use mind power to make people or objects levitate. The closest most people come to levitating is floating in a swimming pool!

HOW TO DO MAGIC

WHAT IS THE WORLD'S SMALLEST COUNTRY?

It's a country within a city within a country. Vatican City in Rome, Italy, is an independent country governed by the Roman Catholic Church. The Pope lives there. Its total area is only one fifth of a square mile, a distance you could easily walk.

ITALY

VATICAN CITY

IT WORKS!

HOW TO DO MAGIC

ZIP!

WHAT IS THE WORLD'S LARGEST MAZE?

The world's largest maze is at the Dole Plantation in Hawaii. Its path is made of 11,400 plants and is 3.11 miles long!

What is petroleum made of?

Ancient plants and marine organisms that died millions of years ago. When the sea life decomposed, it was trapped in rocks or buried beneath tons of sand and mud. Over time and under immense pressure, carbon and other substances left behind by these plants and animals formed petroleum—oil. Because it takes so long for petroleum deposits to form, it is likely that humans will one day use up all of the world's oil. Many scientists are already working to find new energy sources to replace it.

OIL!

Why do stars twinkle?

They really don't. Starlight passes through our atmosphere, and that's where the "twinkling" begins. Dust, smoke, and other particles are always dancing about in the atmosphere. All those swirling particles interfere with a star's light. The star appears to dim and brighten. Also, the atmosphere bends, or *refracts*, the light rays. These influences create the special effect we call twinkling.

Who made the Statue of Liberty?

Frederic Bartholdi designed the statue and Alexandre Eiffel (who designed the Eiffel Tower) built the framework. The grand lady with the torch was given to the United States by France as a symbol of friendship. It represents the liberty of living under a free form of government. Constructed and shipped to the United States in parts, the statue was erected on Liberty Island in New York Harbor in 1886. *Liberty Enlightening the World* (her full name) is one of the largest statues in the world. It's more than 151 feet, from the sandals to the top of the torch, and weighs 450,000 pounds.

HOW DOES A FIGURE SKATER SPIN AROUND *SO FAST?*

Changing one type of posture to another increases the "rotation rate," or speed of a spin. Say a skater is spinning with her arms outstretched—then she pulls her arms in close to her body. She's going to spin faster because the *momentum*, or energy, from her limbs is passed on to her body.

I CAN'T SKATE!

I'M DIZZY WATCHING!

WHAT IS A "LIVING FOSSIL"?

A plant or animal that has survived almost unchanged for millions of years. A fish called the coelacanth (SEE-luh-kanth) is a famous example. Until 1938, scientists believed that coelacanths had been extinct for 90 million years; then a living one was caught off the coast of South Africa. Sharks are also living fossils. They appeared more than 360 million years ago, long before dinosaurs.

I DIDN'T LIVE THIS LONG TO FALL FOR THAT OLD TRICK!

What are fossils?

Preserved traces of once-living things. Fossils are often bones but can also be things like teeth, wood, or shell. You can also find fossilized tracks, burrows, skin impressions, and even fossilized pieces of poop, which are called **coprolites** (KAHP-ruh-lites).

Were dinosaurs and humans ever alive at the same time?

No. Dinosaurs lived on Earth from about 245 million years ago until 65 million years ago, when most become extinct. Our first known human ancestors—*Australopithecines*—appeared about 4 million years ago. The first "modern" humans (those with bodies much like ours) did not appear until about 200,000 years ago.

I NEVER SAW A HUMAN!

DINOSAUR? WHAT'S THAT?

Who was Charles Darwin?

Charles Darwin (1809-1882) was a naturalist (a scientist who studies the natural world). In 1859, he published *The Origin of Species*, a book that presented the theory of evolution—the idea that all plant and animal life gradually change in form, adapting to suit their environment. Darwin's ideas caused a major shift in how people view the world, and sparked debates that continue to this day.

How do we know what dinosaurs looked like?

From finding fossilized dinosaur bones and fitting them together. Scars on dinosaur bones are an important clue: They show how muscles were attached. Experts reconstruct the shape of the muscles, giving us a "picture" of what the dinosaur looked like. Skin impressions from some dinosaur fossils help scientists guess at skin texture and color, based on their knowledge of dinosaurs and living reptiles.

Pterosaurs were flying reptiles, not dinosaurs.

Do sun dogs bark?

No. Sun dogs are bright spots of light appearing on one or both sides of the sun. They are caused by sunlight passing through ice crystals in the air.

Why is the sky blue?

Molecules and dust particles in Earth's atmosphere scatter sunlight. Short light waves, such as violet and blue, scatter better than long red and orange light waves. The blue color that we see is a mix of blue, violet, green, and tiny amounts of other colors scattered across the sky. If you were standing on the moon, which does not have an atmosphere to catch and scatter light, the sky would look black.

What is a rainbow?

When sunlight shines through raindrops, it bounces off the back wall of each drop. When light exits these drops, it splits into different colors because each light wave leaves at a slightly different angle. All raindrops alter light this way. From a distance, our eyes see each color as arcs, or bows, in the sky.

What are the northern lights?

Shimmering, brightly colored bands of light that appear in the night sky near the magnetic north pole. They are caused by particles streaming from the sun, which make gases in Earth's upper atmosphere glow. The best places to see the northern lights—also called the aurora borealis—are northern Alaska, Canada's Hudson Bay, northern Norway, and northern Siberia. Southern lights—called the aurora australis—can be seen near the magnetic south pole.

Barrow, ALASKA

WOW! IT'S HUGE!

Can you see rainbows at night?

Yes. Bright moonlight shining through falling water creates an effect known as a "moonbow," which usually is much fainter than a rainbow. Cumberland Falls in Kentucky is famous for its moonbows.

DO FLYING FISH AND FLYING SQUIRRELS REALLY FLY?

No. They are gliders, not true fliers. Flying fish leap out of the water to escape predators, gliding for short distances on their long front fins. A flying squirrel has a thin membrane of skin that connects its front and back legs. When it leaps from a tree and spreads its limbs, the membrane acts like a parachute, helping it glide safely to the ground.

Is there such a thing as a flying fox?

Yes, but it's not a real fox. Some large bats have brown fur, pointed ears, and a foxy-looking nose. Because of these features, these bats are known as flying foxes. Flying foxes eat fruit or flower nectar and live where it is warm all year.

I DON'T FEEL LIKE FLYING TODAY! I'M TIRED.

What is the BIGGEST flying insect?

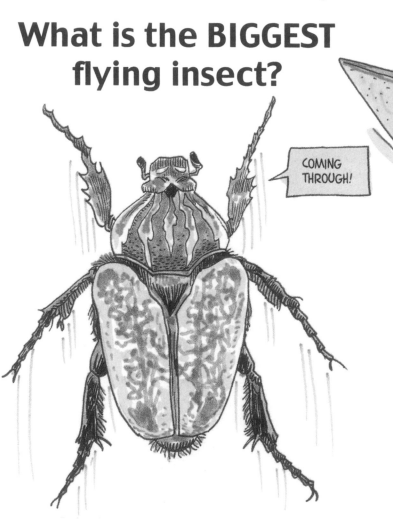

COMING THROUGH!

The Goliath beetle, which lives in the African rain forest, weighs 4 ounces. That's as heavy as a quarter-pound hamburger! The Goliath beetle is so strong it can peel a banana with its forelegs!

Why do birds fly in V formations?

To save energy. The first bird's wings break up the wind, and create a current on which following birds can ride. Birds take turns leading the V, or chevron. Scientists calculate that birds flying alone can go only about 90 percent as far as birds flying in Vs. This is important for birds that migrate long distances, such as geese, which travel across entire continents each spring and fall.

WAIT UP!

HAVE A NICE TRIP.

How big is the largest bird that can fly?

If a bird is too heavy, it can't get off the ground. The Kori bustard from Africa must be close to the limit. It weighs about 30 pounds—almost as much as a three-year-old child.

I NEED TO GO ON A DIET.

WHAT WAS QUETZALCOATLUS?

A flying reptile living near the end of dinosaur times and one of the biggest flying creatures ever. Quetzalcoatlus (KET-sol-koh-AT-lus) cruised over what is now Texas on skinny wings that may have spanned nearly 40 feet.

Have the continents always been where they are today?

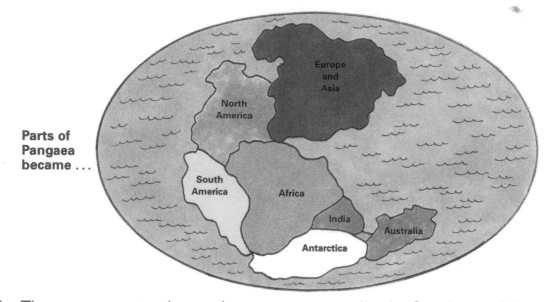

Parts of Pangaea became . . .

North America

Europe and Asia

South America

Africa

India

Australia

Antarctica

No. They are constantly moving—very, very slowly. Sections of Earth's crust, called tectonic plates, shift over time. About 150 million years ago, all of today's continents were joined together in one supercontinent called Pangaea (pan-JEE-uh). But the sea floor spread slowly, pushing them apart. Today, Earth's eight large plates are still moving apart, at the rate of about 2 to 4 inches a year.

What causes EARTHQUAKES?

Tectonic plate

Tectonic plate

As the tectonic plates of Earth's crust move, huge stresses build up in the rocks until, finally, the rocks give way. If this happens in a series of tiny breaks, we don't feel anything, but when that stress is relieved in one big, sudden break, we have an earthquake.

Where is the Valley of Ten Thousand Smokes?

In Katmai (KAT-my) National Monument, Alaska. One of the biggest volcanic eruptions in recorded history occurred here in 1912. Visitors to the valley four years later reported steam rising from tens of thousands of "smokes," or fumaroles— holes in the valley floor near the volcano.

WHAT MADE THINGS ROCK IN NEW MADRID, MISSOURI, NEAR THE END OF 1811?

A series of earthquakes believed to be the strongest in U.S. history shook things up in that area from mid-December 1811 to March 1812. The quakes rattled two thirds of the U.S., changed the course of the Mississippi River, and created new lakes!

What is the San Andreas fault?

California's San Andreas fault is where two huge tectonic plates slide past each other. Hundreds of earthquakes occur here every day, most too small to be felt. During the devastating San Francisco earthquake of 1906, however, land at the San Andreas fault moved about 20 feet in a very short time! In all, there have been more than 160 major quakes in California in the last 100 years.

193

Why does ice float?

Substances are usually most dense when they are solid, because that is when their molecules are most compact. But water is different. Water molecules are farther apart when water is solid (ice) than when it is liquid. This means that ice is less dense than water—so it floats!

LUCKY FOR ME!

What if ice DIDN'T float?

That would be bad news for fish! Lakes and other bodies of water would freeze solid from the bottom up. We wouldn't have the same kinds of aquatic life that we do now, because aquatic animals wouldn't survive winter.

YIKES! LET'S NOT EVEN DISCUSS THE POSSIBILITY!

What is the temperature when it is absolutely the coldest it can get?

Absolute zero, or -459.67 degrees Fahrenheit. Scientists have been able to get within two millionths of a degree of this point in labs. Nothing moves at this temperature, not even a molecule!

I'M STILL COLD!

What is permafrost and how can it cause problems?

Permafrost is soil that stays frozen even in summer. It is found in places close to the poles, such as Alaska and Siberia. Permafrost can cause problems for buildings constructed on it. Warmth can leak through the building's foundation, melting the permafrost, which softens the soil—making it soft enough for the building to sink!

How cold does it get in Antarctica?

The lowest temperature ever recorded anywhere on Earth was -128.6 degrees Fahrenheit at Russia's Vostok research station at the South Pole, on July 21, 1983.

THIS IS MY KIND OF WEATHER!

BRR ... IT'S TOO COLD HERE!

Why do moths circle around bright lights?

Night-flying moths navigate by staying at a constant angle to the moon. If they stick with the moon, they fly in a straight line every time. When they see artificial lights, they get confused and try navigating by them instead, but it doesn't work nearly as well! To keep the light at the same angle, the moth must keep changing direction. It ends up flying in ever-smaller circles around the light.

I'M GETTING DIZZY!

Why don't spiders get stuck in their own webs?

They avoid the sticky sections. Some spiders use dry silk for the web spokes, then lay down a circular pattern of sticky silk around it. The spider runs along the dry silk. If a leg does happen to stick, the spider uses its saliva to dissolve the glue.

How many kinds of beetle are there?

The largest group of insects—by far—are the beetles. Scientists know of about 300,000 different species of beetle, and there probably are many more yet to be identified. The biggest bunch in the beetle world is weevils: The weevil family is more than 50,000 species strong!

Is there really such a creature as a Tasmanian devil?

MAKE MY DAY!

Yes! The real Tasmanian devil is a marsupial (pouched mammal) about 20 to 30 inches long with a foot-long bushy tail. It has a squarish head and a stocky body. This creature's strong teeth and jaws are perfect for tearing apart meat it eats. Today, the only place you can find these little devils in the wild is Tasmania, an island that is part of Australia.

Do animals see COLOR?

Birds seem to be very good at recognizing colors. Most mammals are color-blind, but monkeys, apes, and humans can tell colors apart. Your pet dog or cat probably sees the world in black, gray, and white.

Why don't beavers get SPLINTERS in their mouths?

Mainly, because they don't chew on dry wood. They chew either live trees or water-soaked branches. Also, a beaver's lips close tightly together behind its big front teeth, which locks out bits of wood and also lets the beaver work underwater.

197

What is St. Elmo's fire?

Sometimes, a flamelike mass caused by electricity in the air appears at the tops of tall objects during thunderstorms. Long-ago sailors who noticed this strange light above the masts of their ships named it after their patron saint, St. Elmo. Another name for the fire is *corposant*, a name that means "holy body."

WHAT CAUSES LIGHTNING?

The rapid movement of ice crystals in storm clouds builds up electric charges (similar to the charge that builds up when you rub a balloon on your sleeve). Electric charges also form on the ground beneath the clouds. When a negative charge meets a positive charge, look out! A huge electrical current—a lightning bolt—shoots between the two charges. Most lightning stays up in the clouds; only about a quarter of it strikes the ground.

What is THUNDER?

BARROOOOM!

Lightning heats the air along its path—to temperatures as high as 54,000 degrees Fahrenheit! As it heats, and then cools, this air expands and contracts, forming a series of shock waves that travel at the speed of sound. Our ears pick up those fast-moving waves as the boom, crash, and rumble of thunder.

Why don't electric eels zap themselves?

For the same reason you don't get zapped by the electricity in *your* body! (Electric signals tell your muscles how to move.) Your nerves have a protective coating that shields you against your own electricity, and so do the electric eel's. But the eel's body makes far more electricity than a human's—enough to stun a horse!

HOW CAN BIRDS SIT ON POWER LINES WITHOUT GETTING ELECTROCUTED?

I FEEL GREAT!

ME, TOO!

ME THREE!

A bird sits touching only one line and nothing else through which electricity can flow to the ground—so no current flows through its body. Trying to rescue a kite caught in electric lines is deadly dangerous, however: If a person holds onto a pole and touches a kite caught on a power line, current flows through the kite, into and through the person's body, then to the ground—and the human body cannot absorb such a huge shock.

How can you be moving, even when standing still?

Not only is Earth spinning on its axis at about 1,083 miles per hour, it is also zooming around the sun at more than 65,000 miles per hour. The crustal plate beneath your feet is moving, too—very, very slowly.

GOING UP!

SPINNING 'ROUND!

How big is Earth?

Huge! If we broke Earth into pieces and hauled it away at a rate of 20 tons a second, it would take 1,000,000,000,000,000,000 (that's one quintillion!) years to get rid of the whole planet. Compared to the sun, though, Earth is pretty puny. More than 1 million Earths could fit inside the sun!

THIS WILL TAKE FOREVER!

How much of Earth's surface is water?

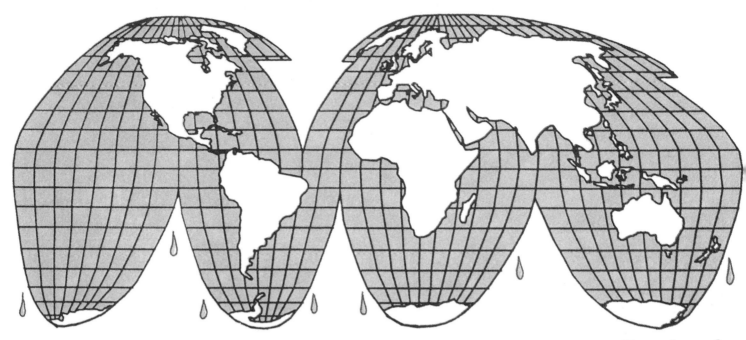

About 70 percent of the surface, or 57,259,000 square miles. Land covers less than one third of the planet's surface. By comparison, the U.S. covers only 2 percent of Earth's surface.

Do hurricanes always spin in the same direction?

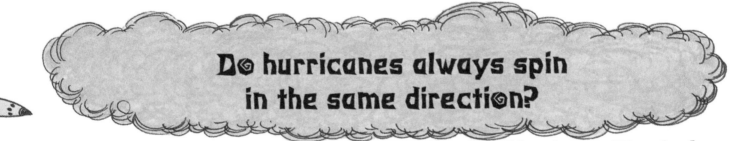

That depends on where you are. In the Northern Hemisphere, hurricanes spin in a counterclockwise direction. In the Southern Hemisphere, the same type of storm, called a cyclone, spins clockwise. That is the *Coriolis* force at work. It is caused by the rotation of Earth, which forces things moving freely across Earth's surface to move on a curved path—including wind and ocean currents.

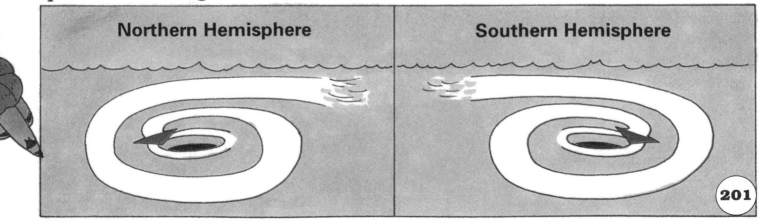

Northern Hemisphere | Southern Hemisphere

Did anybody hear the Big BANG?

No. Most scientists believe that the universe began about 13.5 to 14 billion years ago, with a huge explosion known as the Big Bang. All the matter in the universe began spreading outward from the point of the explosion, and it is still expanding today.

What is a light-year?

The distance that light travels in a year: 5,880,000,000,000 (or about 6 trillion) miles. Scientists use light-years to describe the huge distances between objects in space.

I CAN'T SEE IT YET!

I'LL SHINE MY LIGHT INTO SPACE!

I'M VERY BRIGHT!

What is the brightest star that we can see?

Our sun. It seems brightest because it is so close—only 93 million miles away. Sirius, another star, is about 23 times brighter than the sun but much farther away— 8.6 light-years. Sirius is also larger and hotter than our sun.

How much would you weigh on the moon?

Someone who weighs 100 pounds on Earth would weigh only 17 pounds on the moon. That is because the moon has a low force of gravity. On Jupiter, which has the strongest gravity of all the planets, that same Earthling would weigh a hefty 260 pounds!

I FORGOT TO BRING MONEY!

Check Your Weight in Space!

To find out how much you would weigh on another planet, multiply your weight by the planet's force of gravity. For example, a 100-pound weight on Earth would weigh 120 pounds on Saturn: 100 x 1.2 = 120.

Mercury	0.28	Jupiter	2.6
Venus	0.85	Saturn	1.2
Earth	1.0	Uranus	1.1
Mars	0.38	Neptune	1.4

5¢

What is our galaxy's biggest star?

The Pistol Star. It is 100 times as large as our sun and it burns about 10,000,000,000 times as bright. It unleashes as much energy in six seconds as our sun does in one year. The Pistol Star is invisible to the naked eye because it is hidden 25,000 light-years away behind great dust clouds in the center of our Milky Way galaxy.

How can water break rocks?

I'M A STAMP-STOMPING PACHYDERM!

When water freezes, its molecules expand. So if water gets into a crack in a rock, then turns to ice, it can widen the crack—or shatter the rock entirely. Over thousands of years, this process can turn huge mountains into hilly mounds of gravel. The pressure frozen water exerts on a rock is equal to that of an elephant standing on a postage stamp!

CRACK!

What is hard water?

Hard water has calcium salts, magnesium salts, iron, and aluminum dissolved in it. The more disolved minerals there are in water, the "harder" it is. The harder the water, the more soap you need to work up a lather. Too many minerals dissolved in water can make it taste bad, or be unsafe to drink.

PHOOEY!

UGH!

READER, COULD YOU KINDLY FETCH ME 30 GALLONS OF WATER—NOW?

How can a camel go so long between drinks?

A camel's body does a great job storing water. Camels don't sweat much, and their droppings are dry. A thirsty camel can drink 30 gallons of water in 10 minutes! They also get water from desert plants they eat. All liquid is stored in thick body tissues. When water is scarce, camels use the stored water—losing up to 40 percent of their weight.

WHY DOES STILL WATER ACT LIKE A MIRROR?

All surfaces reflect light. If a surface is smooth and shiny, like still water or a mirror, the light is reflected in an even, orderly way, resulting in a clear image. If the surface is rough, the reflected rays are scattered in different directions, so we don't see a reflected image.

What makes a dry road look wet on a hot day?

Light. What looks like a puddle of water is actually a reflection of the sky. Light rays traveling through cooler air in the sky bend where they meet hot, moist air rising off the road. When light bends, it casts an image of the sky onto the road, just like a mirror.

NICE ICE!

Where is most of the fresh water on Earth?

The ice sheet of Antarctica holds 80 to 90 percent of Earth's fresh water—frozen solid. That ice sheet is an average of 7,100 feet thick! (At its thickest point, it is 3 miles deep!) If it ever melted, the sea level around the world would rise by 180 to 200 feet.

Who were the first people to notice the island of Surtsey being born?

Fishermen. One day in 1963, they noticed something that looked like a rock in the ocean near Iceland where rocks had not been before. A volcano was erupting there, under the sea. As the lava spilled and cooled into rock, it piled higher and wider. Only four days after Iceland's brand-new island first poked out of the ocean, it was 200 feet high and 2,000 feet long! Today its diameter is 2,500 feet.

HOW DO VOLCANOES CAUSE COLORFUL SUNSETS?

Volcanoes often pump large amounts of fine ash into the atmosphere. The ash increases the scattering of sunlight, spreading more red and orange light across the sky. This is especially noticeable at sunset and sunrise, when the sky becomes much more red and purple than usual.

How harmful are tsunamis?

One of the most destructive tsunamis happened in Awa, Japan, in 1703, killing 100,000 people. In 2004, a tsunami devastated the shores of Indonesia, Thailand, Sri Lanka, and southeast India with waves of up to 100 feet, killing more than 200,000 people!

An approaching tsunami may look less dangerous than it really is. In 1755 in Lisbon, Portugal, people went to gaze at the seafloor that had been exposed by a tsunami far out at sea. Many were washed away soon afterward, when the huge wave hit.

What caused a big boom in 1883?

The volcano of Krakatoa in Indonesia. Eruptions began on August 26, but the biggest explosion came the next day, when nearly the entire island was blown to bits. Steam and ash shot 22 miles into the air, and tsunamis sank ships and killed at least 36,000 people. People could hear the explosion almost 3,000 miles away.

What is a geyser?

A hole in the ground from which steam, gas, and hot water spray into the air. Geysers occur in volcanic areas. **Magma** (melted rock from Earth's core) rises close to the surface, where it heats rocks. Those rocks heat water pooled underground. As that water reaches the boiling point, pressure builds until it shoots from the ground.

WHERE DO YOU FIND STALACTITES AND STALAGMITES?

In limestone caves. They are spikelike rock formations caused by dripping water that deposits minerals. Here's a trick to tell which is which: A stalactite (with a c) grows down from the ceiling. A stalagmite (with a g) grows up from the ground.

What are atoms?

Tiny building blocks of matter. Every atom is made of some combination of protons, neutrons, and electrons. Atoms of similar structure make up elements such as oxygen, hydrogen, and helium. These are found in nature, and often team up with other elements to form entirely new substances such as water. Two atoms of hydrogen and one atom of oxygen, for instance, make one molecule of water.

HYDROGEN ATOMS

OXYGEN ATOM

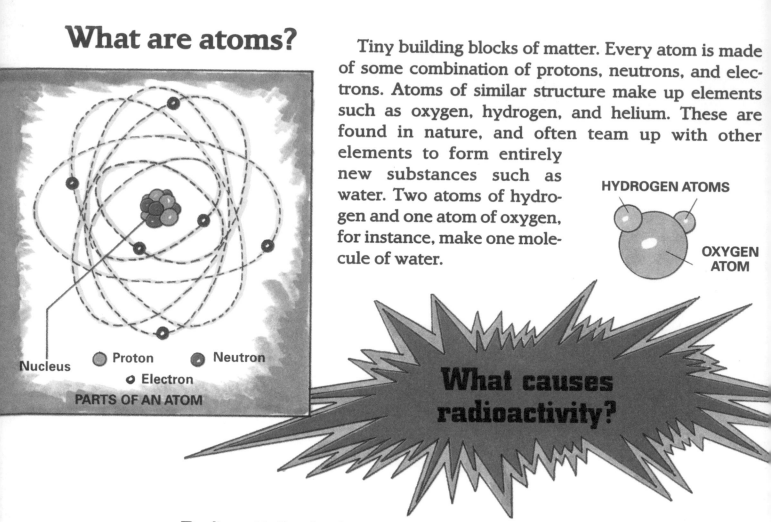

Nucleus

● Proton ● Neutron
◐ Electron

PARTS OF AN ATOM

What causes radioactivity?

Radioactivity is the energy given off by unstable atoms as they change to a more stable form. This energy can be in the form of heat or light. (The light may not be visible to the human eye.)

What is a nebula?

A gigantic cloud in space, made of gas and dust. A nebula (NEB-yoo-luh) can be dark or bright, depending on whether the particles it contains absorb light or reflect it. Some nebulae are bright because they contain hydrogen and helium gases, which glow. Scientists think that nebulae eventually condense to form stars.

How does the sun make light?

By changing lots of hydrogen to helium. Incredibly high temperatures and pressures at the sun's center set off a fusion reaction: Four hydrogen atoms cram together to make one helium atom. But not all the hydrogen is used. Leftovers are converted to a form of heat and light energy that we call sunshine.

WHAT IS SOLAR WIND?

STOP PUSHING!

Bits of atoms—electrons, protons, and some nuclei (NOO-klee-eye)—that the sun's heat speeds up, until they are moving so fast that they escape from the sun's gravity and stream outward. Did you know that a comet's tail always points away from the sun? That is because it is being pushed by solar winds!

Is Saturn the only planet with rings?

Neptune

Uranus

Jupiter

Saturn

No. The planets Jupiter, Uranus, and Neptune also have rings. The gravities of all these planets are strong enough to attract, capture, and hold the dust, chunks of rock, ice, and frozen gas contained in the rings.

What is the Milky Way?

Our home galaxy. We live in the Milky Way galaxy, a flat, spiral galaxy about 100,000 light-years across. Earth is located about 30,000 light-years from the galaxy's center. When we see the hazy band of light called the Milky Way in the night sky, we are seeing the edge of our galaxy.

Who named the constellations?

Ever since people first thought that they could recognize shapes in groups of stars, they have been naming those groups of stars, or constellations. Different cultures use different names for the same constellations. Most of the names that we use, such as Andromeda and Orion, are those of characters in Greek and Roman myths.

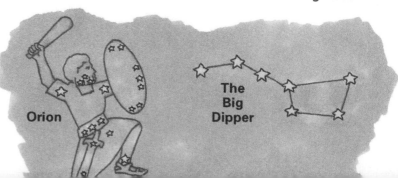

Orion

The Big Dipper

When is Halley's comet coming back?

In the year 2061. The orbit of this famous comet, named after English astronomer Edmond Halley, brings it close to the sun and Earth about every 76 years. Its last appearance was in 1986. American writer Mark Twain was born in 1835 when the comet was in the sky—and died in 1910 on the comet's next visit.

What is an eclipse?

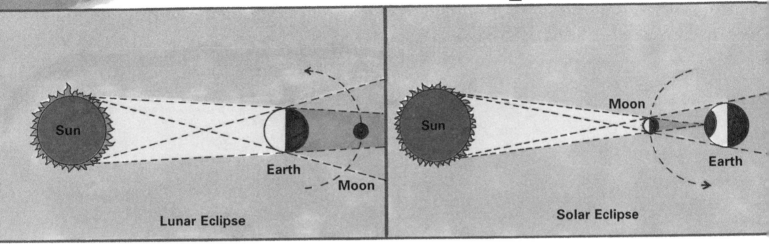

Lunar Eclipse

Solar Eclipse

There are two kinds of eclipses.
*A **lunar eclipse** happens when Earth moves between the moon and the sun, casting Earth's shadow on the moon, which makes it seem to disappear.*
*A **solar eclipse** occurs when the moon passes between Earth and the sun, blocking our view of the sun. The moon's shadow falls on Earth, making the sky dark during the day. For people inside that shadow, the sun seems to disappear.*

Why does the ocean have tides?

As Earth rotates, the moon's gravity tugs on the waters, creating a bulge on each side of Earth. When that bulge occurs near us, we see it as a high tide. When water has flowed away toward bulges elsewhere, we have a low tide. (There are two high tides and two low tides each day.) The highest tides, called spring tides, happen when the sun and the moon line up, both pulling in the same direction.

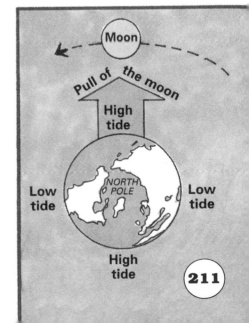

211

What happens along the U.S. Continental Divide?

Water flows toward either the Atlantic Ocean or the Pacific Ocean. The Continental Divide is an imaginary line in the Rocky Mountains that marks where drainage changes from Pacific-bound rivers on the west side of the line, and Atlantic-bound rivers on the east.

What kind of snow is best for making snowballs?

Snowflakes that form at temperatures close to freezing are bigger and wetter than those that form when temperatures are colder than freezing. Wetter snow is stickier than drier snow, so it makes better snowballs— and snowmen!

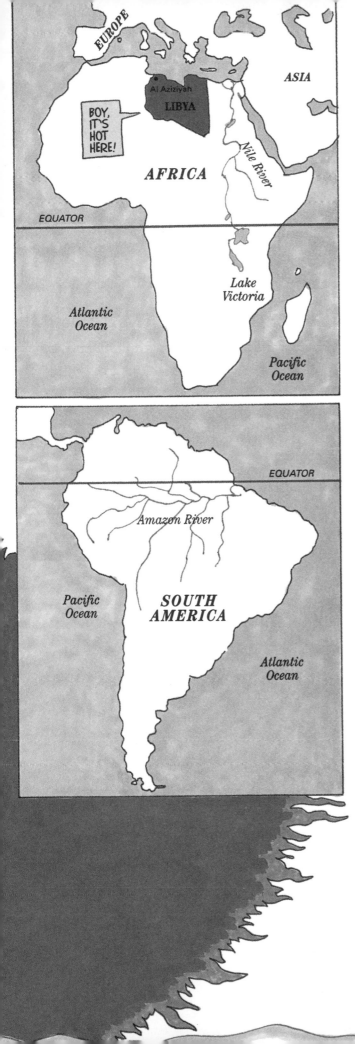

The map shows:
EUROPE
ASIA
Al Aziziyah
LIBYA
BOY, IT'S HOT HERE!
AFRICA
Nile River
EQUATOR
Lake Victoria
Atlantic Ocean
Pacific Ocean

EQUATOR
Amazon River
Pacific Ocean
SOUTH AMERICA
Atlantic Ocean

What Is the HIGHEST TEMPERATURE ever recorded on Earth?

On September 13, 1922, the thermometer read 136 degrees Fahrenheit in Al Aziziyah, Libya. (Actually, it read 57.7 degrees Celsius.)

What is the world's longest river?

The Nile River in Africa is generally considered the longest, measuring 4,160 miles from its source to the Mediterranean Sea. Some say it's the Amazon River in South America, which has many different channels as it nears the Atlantic Ocean, but its length is usually measured at 4,000 miles.

WHERE IS THE WORLD'S SUNNIEST PLACE?

The South Pole during summertime in the Antarctic. All that sunshine doesn't melt the snow and ice, because the ice and snow reflect 50 to 90 percent of it right back into space. It doesn't get very warm there, either—it rarely reaches 32 degrees Fahrenheit, even on a "hot" summer day.

Where can you find black smokers and giant tube worms?

Under the sea. Black smokers are big vents on the deep-ocean floor—about 8,000 feet down—that pump out extra-hot water and chemicals. Living near the smokers are some weird animals, including giant tube worms up to 5 feet long.

I'M A GULPER EEL. I LIVE DOWN HERE, TOO!

Can you find a mermaid's purse on the beach?

AH! THERE'S MY PURSE!

Yes. *Mermaid's purse* is the name for leathery rectangular cases that hold the eggs of skates, rays, and dog-fish. The cases protect the eggs for six to nine months until they hatch. Purses found on the beach are usually empty.

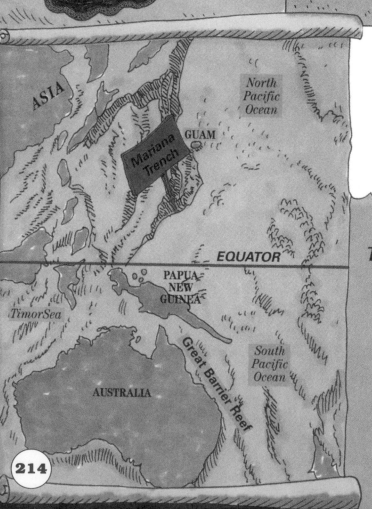

ASIA

North Pacific Ocean

GUAM

Mariana Trench

EQUATOR

PAPUA-NEW GUINEA

TimorSea

Great Barrier Reef

South Pacific Ocean

AUSTRALIA

How DEEP is the ocean?

The deepest ocean, the Pacific, averages about 13,740 feet in depth. The Mariana Trench, in the Pacific Ocean near Guam, is the deepest spot in that ocean—35,840 feet deep. That's more than 6 miles down!

THANKS, MR. COUSTEAU!

WHO WAS JACQUES-YVES COUSTEAU?

Cousteau (1910–1997) was a French inventor, oceanographer, and filmmaker. In 1943, he and engineer Emile Gagnan invented the aqualung, gear that allows divers to stay underwater for long periods of time. His films about undersea life helped millions of people around the world appreciate the beauty and value of the undersea world—and understand the importance of preserving it.

What deadly hunter lives inside a beautiful seashell?

The cone snail. This soft-bodied animal, which lives inside a shell, shoots a poison-tipped tooth into its prey. Poison from some of the larger cone snails is strong enough to kill humans.

The cone snail's stinger sticks out of its shell.

Why are fish slimy?

For protection. The slippery slime makes it tough for parasites to hook on to a fish's body. Slime also protects fish from harmful bacteria, fungi, and algae. Fish continually make new slime and shed the old, along with any nasty things stuck in it.

I'M AS SLIPPERY AS AN EEL!

I'M A TRIGGER FISH.

I'M A ROCK BASS.

I'M A SEA RAVEN.

HOW LARGE IS THE BIGGEST FISH?

The world's biggest fish is the whale shark. It grows up to 40 feet long, or more, and can weigh up to 33,000 pounds! It starts off small, though: A whale shark egg is about 12 inches long, 5.5 inches wide, and 3 inches thick.

What do grunion do at night on California beaches?

On certain spring and summer nights, grunion—a kind of small silvery fish—ride the waves onto the beach. Between waves, the females lay eggs in the sand and the males fertilize them. Then the fish ride the next wave out. The eggs hatch 15 days later, when there is another tide high enough to carry the young grunion away.

WHAT CAUSES WAVES?

Usually, wind blowing over the water. The stronger the wind, or the bigger the stretch of water it blows over, the bigger the waves will be. Tides and earthquakes can also stir up water to make waves.

Whose eerie song might you hear in the ocean?

A humpback whale's. A humpback's song sounds like roars, squawks, and sighs to the human ear. A single song can last 30 minutes, and some parts are repeated—just like choruses in our songs. Songs sung by Atlantic humpback whales are different from those of their Pacific relatives.

How much salt is in the ocean?

We don't know, exactly—but scientists estimate that if you took all the salt from the oceans and spread it evenly, it would form a 500-foot-thick layer over the entire Earth.

Is there a fish that uses a fishing rod?

Yes. The anglerfish uses one to do its fishing deep in the ocean. Growing from its forehead is a thin rod that ends in a glowing bump. The anglerfish sits still and jiggles that lure. Any fish that investigates the lure is quickly gulped down. Some anglerfish can even pull their lure close to their mouth for easier chomping!

YOU SHOULD HAVE SEEN THE ONE THAT GOT AWAY!

What can looking at clouds tell us?

You can "read" clouds the same way you read books. Cloud shapes and sizes are clues to various kinds of weather. For instance, the high, light, puffy clouds, called cumulous clouds, usually accompany good weather. Low, dark, heavy-looking clouds, called altostratus and nimbostratus clouds, are likely to signal a long, steady rain or snowfall. To learn more, keep your eyes on the sky!

IF YOU LIKE THE SOUND OF RAIN, WHERE WOULD BE A GOOD PLACE TO LIVE?

IT'S STILL RAINING.

You might try Mawsynram, India: An average of 467.5 inches of rain falls there every year! Tutunendo, Colombia, would be another choice; it gets 463.4 inches annually. And one year, Cherrapunji, India, was soaked with 1,041.75 inches of rain! (That's higher than an eight-story building!)

Are raindrops really shaped like teardrops?

No. No matter how often we see raindrops drawn that way, the real thing looks quite different. A raindrop looks more like a doughnut or bagel in which the hole doesn't go all the way through. The surface tension of water makes it take this shape.

What is hail?

Hail forms when water droplets are repeatedly swept upward into the cold part of storm clouds where they freeze, then drop back down to pick up more moisture. It takes strong winds to keep hailstones circulating in storm clouds.

CAN I BORROW YOUR SCARF?

OUCH!

How BIG can hailstones get?

WOW!

Most are less than half an inch across, but some can be the size of softballs or larger. The largest hailstone on record, which fell in Bangladesh in 1986, weighed 2.25 pounds!

Do any plants eat meat?

Yes, but they gobble bugs, not humans. The Venus flytrap and other meat-eaters sprout traps that shut when insects trip them. Some trap prey with glue. Others drown insects in slippery-sloped water traps.

Do whales eat big fish?

Most toothed whales eat fish, but their diets do vary. The sperm whale, for instance, eats mainly giant squid, but also fish, octopus, and skate, a relative of the stingray. The orca gobbles up seals, penguins, and other whales! And many other whales, in particular the huge blue whale, eat tiny shrimplike animals called krill. They certainly eat their fill of krill—up to four tons a day!

How is a snake able to swallow something larger than its head?

The top and bottom of a snake's jaws are held together with ligaments that stretch like rubber bands. The left and right halves of the lower jaw can spread apart, and the whole jaw can drop downward to open the snake's mouth really wide.

How do hummingbirds eat on the fly?

SNACK TIME!

Hummingbirds survive on a high-sugar substance called nec- tar. To get it, a hummer sticks its long beak down inside a flower, then rolls its long tongue into a tube to suck up the nectar— all the while batting its wings 50 to 75 times a second.

DINNER TIME!

OOPS!

What do bats eat?

Most bats eat flying insects. Some catch fish, snare spiders and scorpions, or even feast on frogs, lizards, birds, and other bats. Fruit is a favorite with some bats, while others eat flower pollen and nectar. The vampire bat, of course, prefers only the blood of its prey.

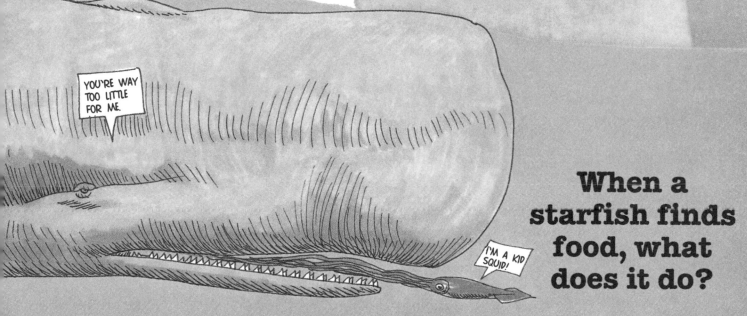

YOU'RE WAY TOO LITTLE FOR ME.

I'M A KID SQUID!

When a starfish finds food, what does it do?

The starfish shoves its stomach outside its body and over the food. Then it eats and digests the food before pulling its stomach back inside. A starfish eats animals that move very slowly or tend to lie still, such as snails, clams, and oysters.

IT'S LUNCH TIME!

CAN PORCUPINES THROW THEIR QUILLS?

WANT A HUG?

No. Porcupines often spin around very fast in order to present their quill-filled backsides to an enemy. The quills are loosely attached to the porcupine's skin and barbed at the tip. Just brushing against these tips is enough to get stuck. The average porcupine has 25,000 to 30,000 quills.

Do hedgehogs have quills when they are born?

I'M NO BABY!

Sort of. The quills are buried just beneath the baby hedgehog's skin, which is puffed up with fluid so the quills don't poke through. Not long after birth, the baby's body absorbs the fluid and small white quills poke through its skin.

How hard can a shark bite?

GULP!

YOU WERE TASTY!

The dusky shark can chomp down with the pressure of 18 tons per square inch—the weight of four adult elephants standing on your thumb! That's about 25,000 times more powerful than an average human's bite!

What surprise is waiting for an animal that grabs a bombardier beetle?

A hot shot. When the bombardier beetle is under attack, chemicals inside its body mix in a special chamber to make a boiling-hot, stinky liquid. The beetle takes aim with its rear end and sprays its attacker.

Why do wasps sting?

RUN, FEET!

They are usually saying "leave me alone!" Wasps will sting to defend their nest from predators or anyone else who disturbs it. Some wasps sting caterpillars to paralyze them, then lay their eggs in the caterpillar's flesh. When the tiny wasps hatch, the caterpillar's body provides them with food.

BUG OFF!

What are the strangler fig's victims?

UGH!

Other plants. Some kinds of fig trees, known as strangler figs, climb up and around other trees, while their roots grow downward. After a while, the fig tree's roots form a thick mat that chokes the life out of the host plant.

WHAT DO SPITTING SPIDERS SPIT?

Something like glue. These spiders spray a sticky, gummy fluid all over their prey, rendering the victim immobile. Splat!

UH-OH!

How does the archerfish get its meals?

UH-OH!

By spitting. This fish lurks underwater, watching for insects on overhanging leaves or grass growing just above the water. When the archerfish spots one, it spits a stream of water droplets, knocking the insect into the water where it can be gobbled up. The fish can shoot a stream five feet high!

PTOOEY!

Which poisonous snake spits?

Africa's spitting cobra. It aims its venom at an enemy's eyes, sometimes shooting while still 10 feet away. The venom either immobilizes the cobra's prey or wards off a potential attacker. If the venom gets in a human's eyes, it causes burning and even temporary blindness.

Do vampire bats really suck blood?

I VANT TO DRINK YOUR BLOOD!

No. Using its razor-sharp teeth, the bat makes a small cut in its prey's skin. The bat licks blood as it oozes from the cut. A chemical in its saliva keeps blood from drying—and numbs skin so victims don't feel a thing. No, vampire bats don't attack humans!

How does a tokay gecko keep its eyes clean?

By licking them. This reptile has no eyelids, so it uses its tongue to moisten and clean its eyes.

THAT'S RUDE!

YOU TELL HIM!

Why do snakes stick out their tongues?

A snake's tongue picks up small particles from the air and ground, and carries them to two pits in the roof of the snake's mouth. Nerves in these pits carry smell and taste information about the particles to the snake's brain, helping it identify its surroundings and track prey.

How do diamonds form?

Diamonds are made from carbon, the same element that makes up the graphite in pencil lead. Diamonds form in a kind of rock called kimberlite, about 75 miles below Earth's surface. The tremendous pressure there helps transform it into the crystals known as diamonds. Diamonds are the hardest known natural substance.

THIS IS NOT WHAT I HAD IN MIND!

Where does soil come from?

Soil is a mix of rotting plant and animal material, and bits of rock from underlying bedrock. This mixes with air and water to provide a home for bacteria, fungi, and tiny plants. There are three major types of soil: clay, silty, and sandy. The bedrock determines the type, but climate, plants, and landscape also make a difference. Soil protects the roots of growing plants and carries nutrients they need in order to grow.

What are the three main kinds of rocks?

Igneous, sedimentary, and metamorphic. Igneous rocks form from **magma** (molten rock). Sedimentary rocks form from layers of sand and mud that settle at the bottom of bodies of water. Metamorphic rocks begin as igneous or sedimentary rocks, but are changed by high temperature and pressure into a new form.

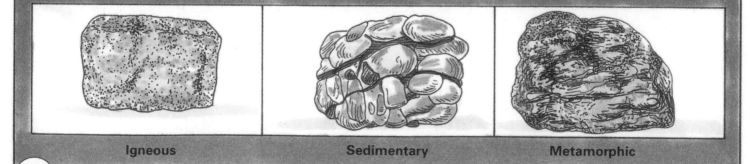

Igneous   Sedimentary   Metamorphic

How BIG is the Grand Canyon?

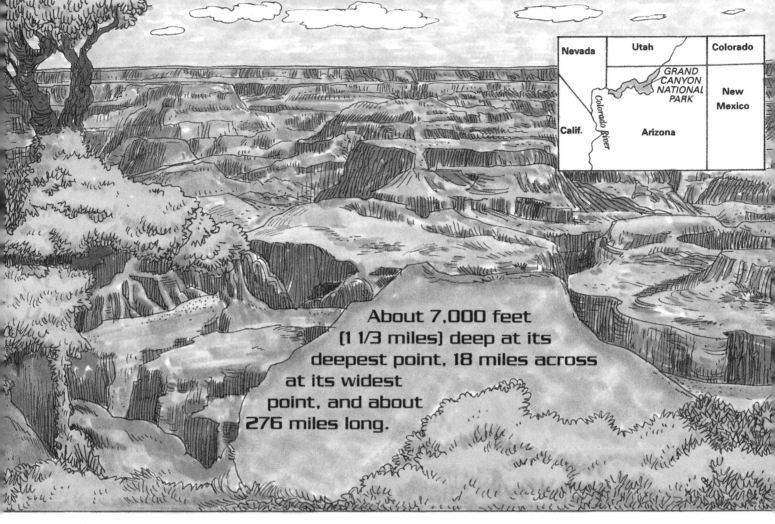

About 7,000 feet
(1 1/3 miles) deep at its
deepest point, 18 miles across
at its widest
point, and about
276 miles long.

Will Niagara Falls always exist?

No. The falls exist now because a layer of hard rock called dolomite lies on top of softer rocks, preventing the Niagara River from wearing them away quickly. But as the soft rocks at the base of the falls wear away, the dolomite collapses, causing the falls to move slowly upstream. Eventually, over hundreds of thousands of years—perhaps even millions of years—the falls will disappear into Lake Erie.

Does anything live in the Dead Sea?

Not much, except for some specialized bacteria and plants. The Dead Sea is really a "terminal" lake—water flows into it, but none flows out. As water evaporates, it leaves behind the salt it contained. The water that is left gets saltier and saltier. The Dead Sea is about eight times as salty as the Atlantic Ocean! By comparison, the Great Salt Lake, in northern Utah, is only three to five times as salty as the ocean.

MMMA!

How do coral reefs form?

A coral polyp is a tiny animal that builds a hard outer skeleton. When a polyp dies, it leaves behind its skeleton. Other polyps build on top of it; and still others grow on top of them. In warm, shallow seas over thousands of years, billions of these tiny skeletons form a coral reef.

Where do pearls come from?

Pearls form when foreign matter, such as a piece of sand, gets inside the shell of an oyster or mussel, irritating the animal's soft body. To protect itself, the shellfish coats the object with layers of a smooth, hard substance called nacre (NAY-ker). In time, as layers build up, the coated object becomes a pearl.

OUCH! SAND JUST GOT INSIDE MY SHELL!

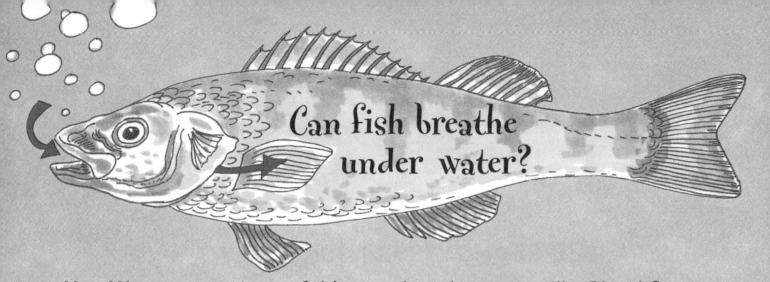

Can fish breathe under water?

Yes. Water passes into a fish's mouth and over its gills. Blood flowing through the gills absorbs oxygen in the water. At the same time, the blood releases carbon dioxide, which is waste, into the water.

HOW DOES A PORCUPINE FISH ESCAPE FROM ITS ENEMIES?

Before

By gulping water or air. The porcupine fish swells into a ball, and its normally flat-lying spines stick straight out. That makes the fish look too big and prickly for most predators to swallow.

After

What do dolphins and some bats have in common?

Both use echolocation to find their prey. They send out sound waves in the form of high-pitched shrieks, which bounce off objects. Returning echoes tell them the direction and distance of things they can't see. With echolocation, the greater horseshoe bat can catch moths in flight and a dolphin can single out a fish from a whole school of them. Dolphins and some bats also use echolocation to help find their way around.

Are all deserts hot and sandy?

No. A desert is a place that gets less than 10 inches of rain a year, often much less. So a desert may be hot and sandy, but it also may be rocky, dusty, or even very cold—as it is in Antarctica, for instance.

Why is xeriscaping a good idea in dry climates?

Xeriscaping (ZEER-uh-SKAPE-ing) is landscaping that doesn't need much water. Xeriscapers use plants that are suited for dry areas, and water them with drip-irrigation systems that lose much less water to evaporation than regular sprinklers do.

Which insects build air-conditioned homes?

Termites. Inside a termite mound, hot air rises into porous-walled chimneys at the top. There, carbon-dioxide waste and heat escape to the outside, while oxygen comes in from the outside. The cooler, oxygenated air sinks into the mound, where the colony lives.

THIS IS GOING TO BE COOL!

WHY DON'T CACTI HAVE LEAVES?

Most plants rely on their leaves to make food, but a plant's water supply can evaporate quickly from a leaf's broad surface. Cacti, which live mainly in areas where water is scarce, have no leaves, but make food in their stems instead. A cactus stem also acts as a water barrel, allowing some large cacti to store tons of water.

Where would you look for living stones?

In the South African desert. A living stone is a type of plant similar to cacti. Each plant has two big, round, swollen, waxy leaves stuck together. The leaves, which are colored like pebbles, blend in with the plant's surroundings.

Where is the largest thing on Earth ...

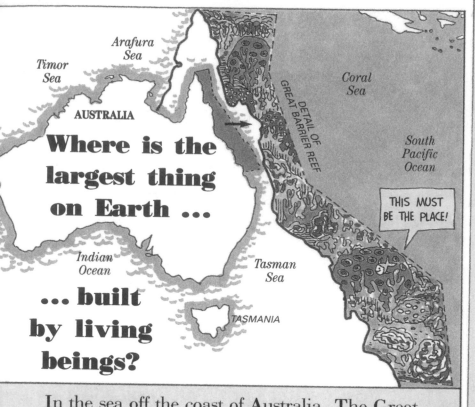

... built by living beings?

In the sea off the coast of Australia. The Great Barrier Reef, which is made of coral, is 1,250 miles long and occupies about 80,000 square miles.

How do crickets sing?

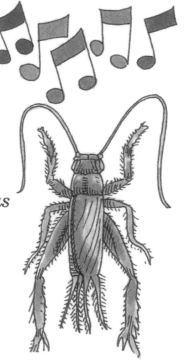

*By rubbing their wings together. One wing has a row of bumps that look like the teeth on a comb; the other wing is edged with tough tissue. When the toughened edge hits a bump, it makes a click that is **amplified** (made louder) by another part of the wing. Only male crickets sing.*

Are humans the only animals that use tools?

No. Chimpanzees poke twigs into termite nests, then eat the insects that cling to the twig when it is pulled out. Egyptian vultures drop stones on ostrich eggs to break them open. Otters balance stones on their bellies, using them to crack open clams and other shellfish. Other animals use tools, too.

What does the trap-door spider do with its trapdoor?

When it is hungry, the spider lurks just under the hinged lid to its burrow, out of sight, waiting to grab prey that wander too close. The same trapdoor also protects the spider from becoming another animal's prey.

How do male bowerbirds advertise for mates?

With decorated display sites called bowers. The male builds two parallel walls of sticks, which he may steal from another bird. Then he adds shells, pebbles, bits of glass, even buttons and coins. Blue feathers are the most popular items.

Why do some orchids look like bees?

To fool bees into spreading their pollen. When the bee tries to mate with what it thinks is another bee, some of the orchid's pollen sticks to it. The bee then carries that pollen to other orchids, fertilizing them.

How do PALEOCLIMATOLOGISTS figure out Earth's past climates?

They use many kinds of clues. Ancient air trapped in Antarctica's ice gives information about the atmosphere long ago. Plant and animal fossils can reveal how warm, cold, wet, or dry it was in the past. Experts called palynologists (pal-ih-NOLL-uh-jists) even study pollen, ancient and modern. By figuring out what plant the tiny fossilized grains came from, palynologists can reconstruct ancient landscapes.

> I CAN'T EVEN FIGURE OUT HOW TO PRONOUNCE IT!*

*Simple! Just say "PAY-lee-oh-KLY-muh-TAHL-uh-jists."

What is the greenhouse effect?

The glass of a greenhouse traps the sun's heat inside. Earth's atmosphere acts like that glass, keeping the planet's surface warmer than it would be otherwise. If it didn't, Earth would be covered with ice. But now scientists worry that we are making it *too* warm. Adding carbon dioxide to the atmosphere, which traps the sun's heat, increases this warming effect. Carbon dioxide gas is a normal part of the atmosphere, but cars, power plants, and other human-made devices give off much more than would occur naturally.

Why are tall mountains often snowcapped?

I LOVE THIS KIND OF WEATHER!

When warm winds hit a mountain, they are forced upward where they cool, and where the moisture they carry forms clouds. The higher you go, the cooler and thinner the air. Warm air hitting a mountain creates the perfect conditions for snow to form and fall on the mountain's peak.

Where was the first real weather-recording station?

CHANGE THAT FROM PARTLY CLOUDY TO RAINY!

Oxford, England. The Radcliffe Observatory there began keeping regular, daily weather records in January 1815, tracking the area's temperature and rainfall. The Radcliffe's archives include older weather records; irregular readings were taken there as far back as 1767.

What happens to a mercury thermometer at -40°F and below?

It becomes useless, because the mercury freezes. To measure temperatures colder than -40°F, scientists use thermometers filled with alcohol, or ones that measure the movement of electrons.

BRRRR!

YIKES! IT'S FROZEN SOLID!

I'M FROM DENVER!

Why does it take longer to hard-boil an egg in Denver than in New Orleans?

Water's boiling point is strongly affected by air pressure, which is lower at high altitudes. Water boils at a lower temperature because of the lower atmospheric pressure. That's why you need more time to boil an egg in Denver, Colorado—nicknamed "the Mile-High City" for it's high altitude—than in New Orleans, Louisiana which is at sea level.

I'M FROM LOUISIANA!

What is the difference between Fahrenheit and Celsius temperatures?

Fahrenheit (F) and Celsius (C) are two different scales that give the same information: the temperature in degrees (°). Water freezes at a certain temperature: 32°F or 0°C. Its boiling point is 212°F or 100°C.

To convert from Fahrenheit to Celsius, take the temperature, subtract 32, multiply by 5, then divide by 9. To convert Celsius to Fahrenheit, multiply the Celsius temperature by 1.8, then add 32.

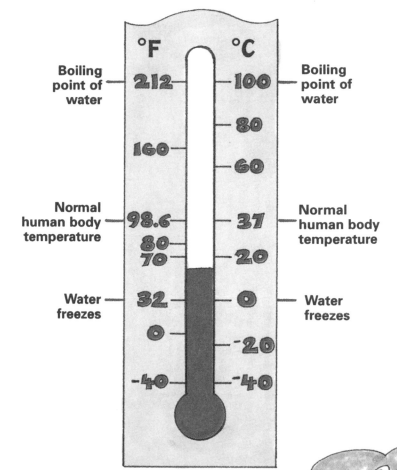

°F		°C	
Boiling point of water	212	100	Boiling point of water
		80	
	160	60	
Normal human body temperature	98.6	37	Normal human body temperature
	80		
	70	20	
Water freezes	32	0	Water freezes
	0		
		-20	
	-40	-40	

Can counting cricket chirps really help you find out the temperature?

Folklore says yes, but there is no scientific basis for this method. Sometimes it works, sometimes it doesn't! If you want to try it, do this: Count how many times a cricket chirps in 14 seconds, then add 40. That is supposed to give you the temperature in degrees Fahrenheit.

READY, SET, COUNT!

How quickly can the temperature change?

Ask anyone who was in Spearfish, South Dakota, on January 22, 1943. That day, the temperature in Spearfish shot up 49° in just 2 minutes (from -4°F to 45°F). Later that same morning, it fell 58°F (from 54°F to -4°F) in 27 minutes! That weather roller coaster was probably caused by cold and warm fronts bouncing off the Black Hills and across the Great Plains.

I'M WARM!

I'M COLD!

What happened to passenger pigeons?

About 200 years ago, some three to five billion passenger pigeons lived in North America. They were overhunted by humans, however, and became extinct. The last passenger pigeon, named Martha, died in 1914. This may have been the only time in history when humans witnessed the precise moment of a species' extinction.

Why did Congress pass the Endangered Species Act?

To protect plants and animals threatened by human activities. This law, passed in 1973, makes any activity that threatens the survival of an endangered species illegal. In North America alone, more than 900 plants and animals are considered endangered.

THANKS FOR PUTTING THE ROCKY MOUNTAIN GOAT ON THE LIST!

Who was John Muir?

Scottish-born John Muir (1838–1914) was one of America's earliest conservationists. He explored California's Sierra Nevada Mountains and Alaska's glaciers, and used his writings to teach people about nature's beauty. At his urging, the U.S. government established Yosemite and Sequoia national parks. Muir also founded the Sierra Club, an organization that continues to support conservation today.

WHAT IS A FOOD CHAIN?

YUM YUM YUM YUM YUM YUM

Eaters being eaten by other eaters. Food chains usually begin with plants, which make their own food. Animals eat the plants, then are eaten by other animals, which are eaten by other animals, and so on. Any break in a food chain can be disastrous to many types of life. For instance, if prairie dogs are killed off by habitat destruction, ferrets that eat prairie dogs will dwindle in number, too. Many different food chains are part of larger food webs—several food chains linked together—because most animals eat more than one kind of food.

WHY ARE SO MANY ANIMALS IN DANGER OF BECOMING EXTINCT?

I'M A TUATARA!

I'M AN ARCTIC FOX.

Extinction is a naturally occurring process but one of the reasons that some species have become extinct is because of humans. Many of the things that humans have built—cities, roads, automobiles, and power plants, for instance—pollute or limit the habitats of animals. The numbers of some wild species are also reduced by hunting.

Threatened species have been saved when people have made an effort to change destructive habits.

I'M A JAGUAR.

Where was the first national park?

In an area that spreads across parts of Idaho, Montana, and Wyoming. In 1872, U.S. President Theodore Roosevelt and the U.S. Congress made this area, named Yellowstone National Park, the first national park in the U.S.—and the world. Today, the U.S. National Park Service oversees 54 national parks, as well as a number of historic sites, seashores, memorials, and other protected sites.

What are fossil fuels?

Fuels made from the remains of plants that lived millions of years ago. Natural gas, coal, and oil are all fossil fuels.

What is air pollution?

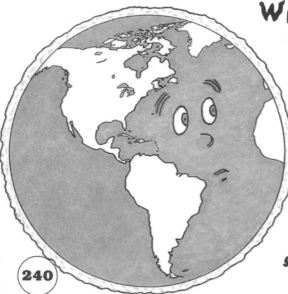

Air that has been tainted by **toxic** (poisonous) chemicals. Many such chemicals are given off when fossil fuels are burned—by car or truck engines, for instance, or by factories or power plants.

Air pollution contributes to water pollution when solid particles of harmful chemicals rise through the air to mix with water particles in clouds, then fall as rain.

What is harming the ozone layer?

Industrial chemicals called chlorofluorocarbons (CFCs) are the biggest culprit. When CFCs get into Earth's upper atmosphere, they break up to form chlorine monoxide and other chemicals that damage the ozone there.

Earth's ozone layer is an important protection against the sun's ultraviolet rays, which are harmful to humans and other forms of life. To protect the ozone layer, many companies now use less-harmful chemicals in aerosol sprays and refrigerants, the main sources of CFCs.

Who was Rachel Carson?

Rachel Carson (1907-1964) was a marine biologist and environmentalist. In 1962, her book *Silent Spring* was published and gained widespread attention. It made many people aware, for the first time, of how humans were polluting the environment with insecticides. Carson wrote other nature books, but *Silent Spring* is regarded as her masterpiece—the book that launched the modern environmental movement throughout the world.

How can pesticides harm birds?

If a bird eats animals that have been exposed to pesticides, the chemicals stay in the bird's body and become concentrated there. Sometimes these chemicals cause a bird to lay eggs with shells that break easily, preventing the eggs from hatching. If the bird absorbs too high a level of the chemicals, it may be poisoned and die. Pesticides almost wiped out peregrine falcons and bald eagles in the eastern U.S.

PESTICIDES RUINED MY EGGS!

What is organic gardening?

A way of growing plants without using chemical pesticides and fertilizers. *Organic* means using natural food or fertilizers rather than chemical ones. Organic fertilizers, such as **compost** (rotted plant material) or fishmeal, are used to enrich the soil. Instead of an insecticide, an organic farmer may use ladybugs to get rid of problem insects. Organic gardening grows crops without hurting the environment.

What is dew?

On cool, cloud-free nights, if the temperature of the ground and other surfaces drops low enough, warm air cools down, condensing moisture contained in it. That moisture collects on cool surfaces in droplets of water called dew.

Why does the Namibian darkling beetle stand on its head?

I'M THIRSTY!

The Namibian darkling beetle lives in the desert, where water is scarce. As it stands on its head, moisture from damp breezes condenses on its shell, forming dewdrops. The drops trickle down to the beetle's mouth, and it drinks them.

Why can you see your breath when it's really cold?

When you exhale in cold weather, the water vapor in your warm breath hits the cold air and condenses into tiny water droplets. Presto: an instant mini-cloud!

HOW DID YOU DO THAT?

What is the driest place on Earth?

WE NEVER GO THERE!

The Atacama Desert in northern Chile. It gets almost no rainfall, except for an occasional shower only several times each century. Rain falls so seldom there that the showers average out to a mere 0.003 inches of rain a year. Now *that* is dry! Another very dry place is the area around the South Pole, in Antarctica. What little moisture there is is locked up solid—frozen into ice.

South Atlantic Ocean

IF YOU'RE GOING TO VISIT HERE, BRING YOUR OWN WATER!

ATACAMA DESERT

C H I L E

South Pacific Ocean

How can a sponge hold water if it's got holes?

The holes in a sponge expose more of the sea creature's absorbent surface, letting it soak up far more water than a sponge with no holes ever could. The first sponges people used were the porous bodies of certain sea animals, but humans later learned how to make artificial sponges.

A

B

C

Three Types of Natural Sponge
A. Purple tube
B. Sulphur
C. Sheepswool

Will fool's gold make you rich?

No way. Fool's gold is pyrite, a mineral that contains iron and sulfur. Prospectors were often fooled into thinking that pyrite was gold because it looks metallic and has a golden color. That is how it got its nickname. Geologists never mistake the two. Gold, one of the heaviest metals, can be pounded into other shapes, stretched into wire, and cut into slices. Pyrite has none of these properties.

Where does amber come from?

Amber is fossilized sap, or resin, from trees that lived about 40 to 60 million years ago. Sometimes the transparent yellow pieces of amber contain insects, leaves, or parts of other living things that were trapped in the sticky sap before it hardened.

What is petrified wood?

A fossil. Over thousands of years, water seeping through buried wood slowly replaces parts of the plant with minerals, such as silica and calcium carbonate. This makes the wood look as if it has petrified, or turned to stone. Sometimes this mineralization is so thorough that the ancient wood is preserved with all of its original details intact. The famous Petrified Forest, located in northeastern Arizona, contains fossilized trees 225 million years old.

ATTENTION, FELLOW WOOD-PECKERS ... DO NOT VISIT THE PETRIFIED FOREST!

What is so interesting about the La Brea Tar Pits?

Their record of prehistoric life. Between 10,000 and 40,000 years ago, many animals became trapped in the pools of sticky tar that oozed from below Earth's surface. Bones of saber-toothed tigers, mammoths, horses, and camels have all been found here, along with plant fossils. This ancient site is in the midst of a modern city—Los Angeles, California.

How was coal formed?

Hundreds of millions of years ago, trees and other plants died in ancient swamps and sank into the water, layer upon layer. As the swamplands sank, seas covered them, laying silt and sand, called sediment, over the decaying plants. As layers of sediment built up, pressure on the plant material increased, forcing out the water and pressing together what was left. Over time, this changed the plant matter into coal.

Peat-forming swamp

Compacted sediments and sedimentary rocks

Compressed peat

COAL

Underclay

How do forest fires start?

Often with a lightning strike. The air at a lightning bolt's center is very hot—as much as five times as hot as the surface of the sun. When that heat meets the wood of a dry tree, it sparks a fire that spreads to other trees. Forest fires are also started by careless campers who fail to put out their fires properly.

Was there really a man called Johnny Appleseed?

Yes. His real name was John Chapman (1774–1845). He traveled throughout the U.S. Midwest, planting apple orchards. He also gave seeds and young trees to pioneers who were headed west, encouraging them to plant their own orchards. By the time he died, he owned many plant nurseries and orchards, and had won fame for starting many others.

Why are *RAIN FORESTS* so important?

ANOTHER RAINY DAY!

YES!

They provide homes for more than half the known (and unknown) plant and animal species on Earth—more than any other habitat. Rain forests are abundant in medicinal plants and rid the air of pollutants. But sadly, humans have cut down much of them. Today the forests cover only two percent of Earth's surface; once, they covered twice that area. The forests are in Central and South America, West and Central Africa, and Southeast Asia.

Who was Smokey the Bear?

ONLY YOU CAN PREVENT FOREST FIRES.

At first, he was just a cartoon character that told people, "Only *you* can prevent forest fires." Then, in 1950, a fire-fighting crew in New Mexico rescued a bear cub from a forest fire. Named Smokey after the cartoon, he lived at the National Zoo in Washington, D.C., serving as a symbol for fire prevention. Smokey died in 1976.

How are fish scales like tree trunks?

Both grow more in spring and summer than in winter. This seasonal growth can be used to calculate fish ages. Fine ridges on the scales are closer in lean years, farther apart in years of abundant food. Scientists can use them to track Earth's cycle of floods, droughts, and diseases.

I'M BIG!

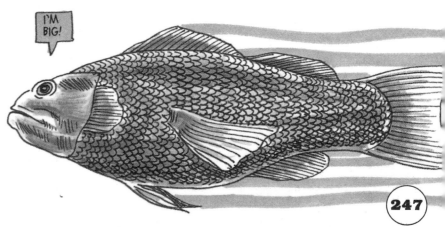

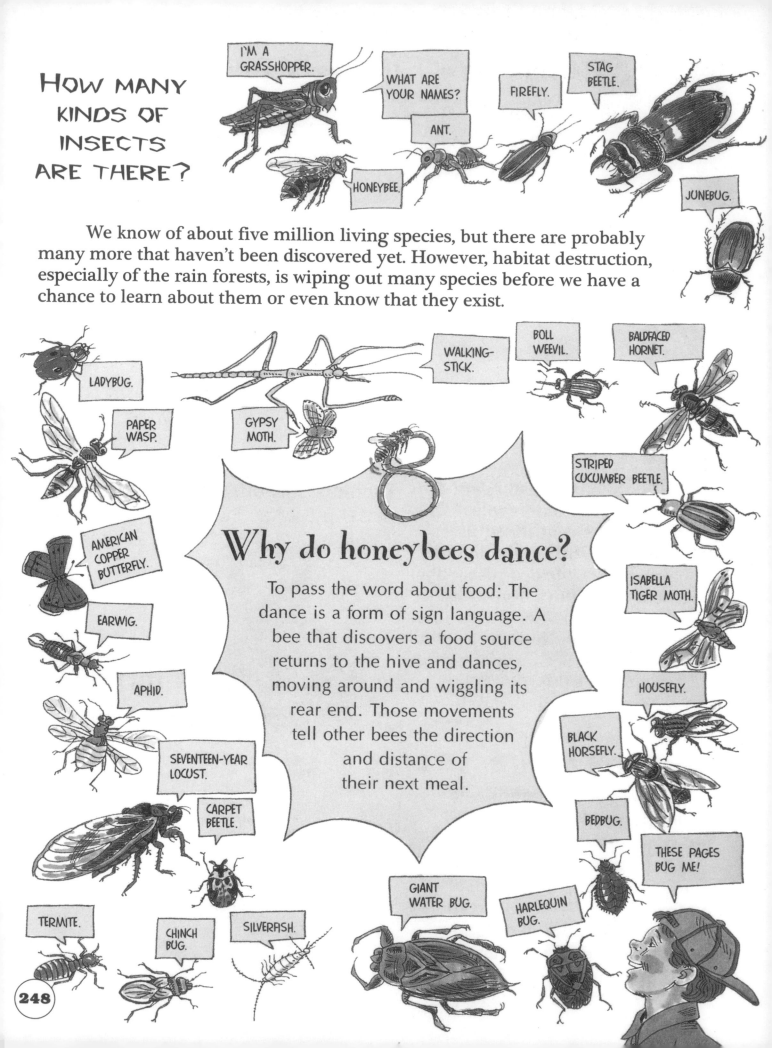

HOW MANY KINDS OF INSECTS ARE THERE?

We know of about five million living species, but there are probably many more that haven't been discovered yet. However, habitat destruction, especially of the rain forests, is wiping out many species before we have a chance to learn about them or even know that they exist.

Why do honeybees dance?

To pass the word about food: The dance is a form of sign language. A bee that discovers a food source returns to the hive and dances, moving around and wiggling its rear end. Those movements tell other bees the direction and distance of their next meal.

Is there an insect that eats animal dung?

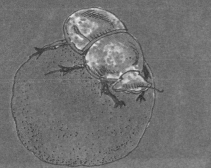

Yes, the aptly named dung beetle. Dung beetles live all over the world—just about anywhere animal dung is found. There are thousands of different species; most eat the dung. Some species roll it into a big ball and lay their eggs in it. It sounds yucky, but dung beetles are vitally important. They help keep planet Earth clean!

Where do dragonflies live until they get their wings?

BEATS ME!

Under water. Young dragonflies, called nymphs (NIMFS), have gills and can breathe underwater. Nymphs are great hunters; they will even capture small frogs or fish. After **molting** (shedding its skin) several times under the water, the nymph climbs out of the water, sheds its skin one last time, and emerges as an adult dragonfly.

Why are some insects born without a mouth?

Because they don't need one! Some male moths live only long enough to mate before dying. They don't have a mouth because eating would waste the precious time they have to further their species.

Which is stronger, spiderweb silk or steel?

Spiderweb silk! You have to pull harder to break a strand of silk than you do to break a steel wire of the same thickness.

What happened at Silver Lake, Colorado, in 1921?

It snowed 76 inches in a single, 24-hour-period! It was not even winter then—that incredible snow-fall occurred in the middle of April!

Almost as bad was the 24-hour snowfall that hit Thompson Pass, Alaska, on December 29, 1955: 62 inches.

I DID NOT KNOW THAT!

What helps the little Arctic fox keep warm?

Its fur, for starters. Arctic fox fur insulates better than that of any other mammal. This fox's short legs, furry feet, and small, round ears help reduce the loss of heat from its body. The Arctic fox's body doesn't have to start working harder to keep it warm until the temperature drops below -40°F.

LISTEN TO THIS!

WHY DOES SNOW SOMETIMES SQUEAK?

When the temperature is 20°F or colder, soft, wet snowflakes turn into hard, rough ice crystals. The squeaking that you hear when you step on the snow is the sound of thousands of those crystals bumping into and sliding past each other.

What happens during an AVALANCHE?

Tons of snow slide down a steep slope. It takes very little to trigger an avalanche: A change of temperature, the weight of new snow, even the weight of a single skier or the slam of a car door can set one off. An avalanche can move faster than 200 miles an hour, burying everything in its path.

Where is it colder, at the North Pole or the South Pole?

The South Pole. It sits on a mountain, where it is colder than at sea level. The North Pole is located on an ice cap floating on the Arctic Ocean. Warmth from the ocean keeps the North Pole's temperature higher than it would be otherwise.

What are pingos?

Soil-covered mounds of ice found in permafrost areas in the Arctic and the interior of Alaska. A pingo is usually circular and may be up to 230 feet tall. At its center is a core of almost pure ice. In Eskimo, pingo means "small hill."

251

What is the windiest place in the U.S.?

Mount Washington, New Hampshire, where the annual average wind speed is 35.3 miles per hour. People at the top, where there is a weather station, are used to breezy days—up there, they regularly get winds of 100 miles an hour.

What is a CYCLONE?

A tropical storm spiraling around a clear, central area called the eye. Only storms with winds higher than 74 miles per hour are called tropical cyclones. This type of storm, found in warm areas, is called a hurricane when it occurs in the Atlantic Ocean or Caribbean Sea; a typhoon when it occurs in the western Pacific. A tropical cyclone may be 600 miles across and carry hundreds of thunderstorms.

Who started naming hurricanes?

I'LL NAME THIS ONE AFTER ME!

For centuries, hurricanes in the Caribbean area were named for the saint's day when they struck. In the late 19th century, Clement Wragge, an Australian meteorologist, started giving hurricanes women's names. Since 1979, the names have been taken from an alphabetical list of both male and female names chosen each year by an international meteorological committee.

WHY DOES THE WIND BLOW?

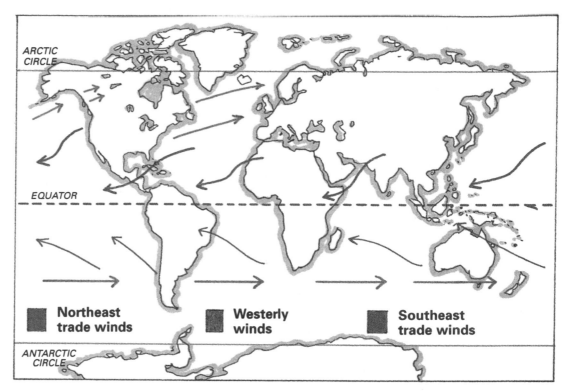

■	Northeast trade winds	■	Westerly winds	■	Southeast trade winds

Because not all the air on Earth is the same temperature. Warm air is lighter than cold air. As warm air rises, cool air flows in to take its place. This movement is what we call wind—nature's way of evenly mixing hot and cold air.

How is a tornado measured?

With the Fujita tornado scale, developed in the late 1960s by Dr. T. Theodore Fujita, a tornado specialist. The scale has six levels:

Scale number	Wind speed	Damage caused
F-0	Up to 72 mph	Light
F-1	73-112 mph	Moderate
F-2	113-157 mph	Considerable
F-3	158-206 mph	Severe
F-4	207-260 mph	Devastating
F-5	261-318 mph	Incredible

What makes flamingoes pink?

WHAT DO FLAMINGO LAWN ORNAMENTS EAT?

Flamingoes get their color from pigments in the food they eat, which includes small fish, insects, and algae. These are similar to the pigments that tint carrots and tomatoes. Flamingoes in zoos may turn white if they are not given the right kind of food.

What makes grass green?

Chlorophyll (KLOR-uh-fill), a bright-green substance found in leaves. Grass, trees, and other leaf-bearing plants use chlorophyll to turn sunlight into energy, in a process called photosynthesis (FOH-toh-SIN-thuh-sis). This is what provides plants with the food they need to grow.

IT SURE IS GREEN!

What makes some animals' eyes shine at night?

Animals that are active at night, such as cats, wolves, and owls, have a shiny layer at the back of their eyes that reflects light upon the part of the eye where images are formed. This lets animals see in very low light. The shine that we see is light reflecting off that layer.

MEOW!   GRRRR!   HOO-HOOT!

How does a chameleon catch food?

YUM!

With its long, lightning-fast tongue. A chameleon's tongue is as long as its body and tail combined, with a sticky pad at the end. When prey appears within striking distance, the tongue darts out, grabs the prey with the sticky pad, then snaps back into the chameleon's mouth—all in less than one second. Now *that's* fast food!

Are all white animals albinos?

HOO! SNOWY OWL, THAT'S WHO!

POLAR BEAR IS MY NAME!

WE ARCTIC HARES ARE WHITE!

YOU CAN CALL ME ARCTIC FOX.

No. True albino animals are white because they lack melanin. Their eyes are pink due to the blood coursing through them. Other animals may be almost entirely white but still have melanin in some areas, such as their noses or eyes.

Why are poisonous animals often brightly colored?

Bright colors work like warning signs that say, "Keep off! I'm dangerous!" to potential predators. If an animal *is* lucky enough to survive eating or attacking one of these creatures, it will always remember that bright colors make for an unpleasant experience.

I'M A COLORFUL CORAL SNAKE.

POISON ARROW FROG, THAT'S ME!

DON'T PET ME! I'M A BLACK WIDOW SPIDER!

255

What makes seasons change?

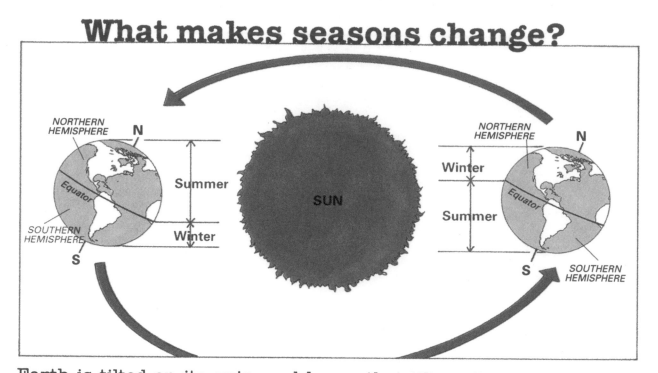

Earth is tilted on its axis, and keeps that tilt as it moves around the sun. When the northern half is tilted toward the sun, it has long, warm summer days, while the south has the short, cool days of winter. On the other side of the sun, the positions are reversed, giving the north winter and the south summer.

Do all trees change color in autumn?

No. Trees that change color with the seasons are called *deciduous*. Trees that stay green all year round are called *evergreen*. Which trees are which may depend on where you live. A species of tree that changes color and loses its leaves in autumn in a cool, northern climate may stay green and leafy all year long in a tropical area, where it is always warm and moist.

What is hibernation?

A strategy to conserve energy when the weather is cold and food is scarce. Some animals, such as black bears, pass each winter curled up asleep in a warm place. Their body temperatures drop and their body processes slow down.

What do snowshoe rabbits and ptarmigan (TAR-mih-gun) do in spring and fall?

Change colors. These animals live in the far north, where winters are long and snowy. As winter approaches, the animals' coloring gradually changes from a mottled brown to a snowy white that blends better with snow. In the spring, it changes back to brown.

Where do butterflies go in the winter?

When the weather starts to get chilly, some butterflies, such as the monarch, migrate to warmer places. Butterflies that stay in cold areas hibernate through the winter, after laying eggs. The eggs hatch, and the offspring spend the winter as caterpillars or in cocoons, where the transformation from caterpillar to butterfly occurs.

Does hay cause hay fever?

Not really. The sneezes and sniffles of hay fever are an allergic reaction to pollen and mold in the air. (Allergies make the body's defensive systems react to harmless substances as if they were dangerous.) Hay fever is worst in spring, when flowers bloom, and in autumn, when mold grows on fallen leaves.

Where is the world's tallest waterfall?

On the Churún River, in a rain-forest area of Venezuela, in South America. Angel Falls drops 3,212 feet from the rim of a mesa to the river valley below. Its longest unbroken drop is a 2,648-foot plunge down a sheer cliff.

HOW HIGH IS THE SKY?

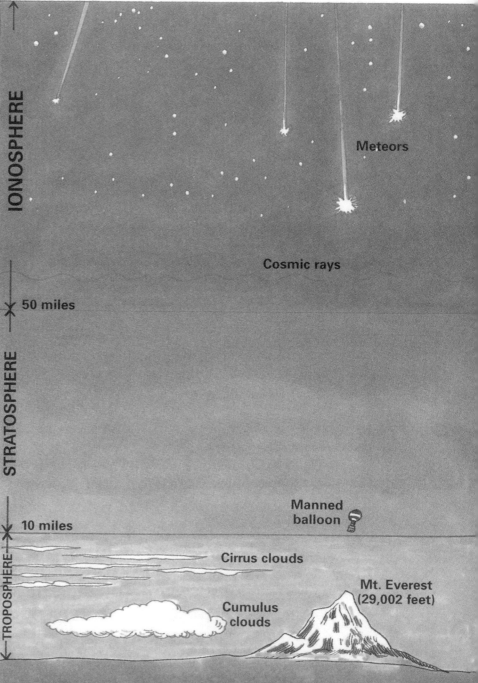

250 miles

IONOSPHERE

Meteors

Cosmic rays

50 miles

STRATOSPHERE

Manned balloon

10 miles

TROPOSPHERE

Cirrus clouds

Cumulus clouds

Mt. Everest (29,002 feet)

The top layer of Earth's atmosphere, called the ionosphere, ends about 250 miles above the planet's surface. The highest clouds lie far below, fewer than 10 miles above the ground.

How fast does a snail move?

When a garden snail is really zipping along, it can manage 0.005 miles (26.4 feet) per hour. Snails crawl on their single foot. A special gland in the foot secretes mucus that lubricates their path.

How many ants are there on Earth?

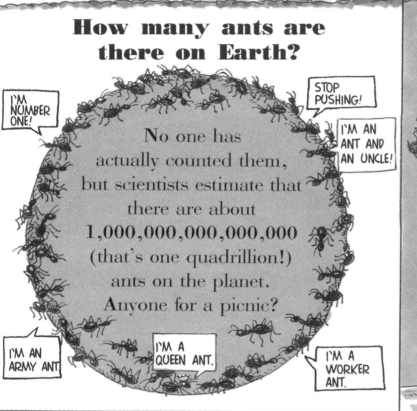

No one has actually counted them, but scientists estimate that there are about 1,000,000,000,000,000 (that's one quadrillion!) ants on the planet. Anyone for a picnic?

What fills the skies over Veracruz, Mexico, each autumn?

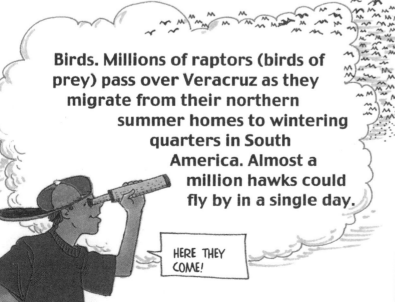

Birds. Millions of raptors (birds of prey) pass over Veracruz as they migrate from their northern summer homes to wintering quarters in South America. Almost a million hawks could fly by in a single day.

Do trees live a very long time?

Some species do. Until recently, bristlecone pines in California were thought to be the oldest, living up to 5,000 years or more. Now super-old spruce trees in Sweden have been found. Some of the above-ground trunks of the trees are younger than the older sections, but the root system of the oldest discovered tree is over 9,550 years old!

What is the difference between a bilby and a bulbul?

A bilby, also known as a rabbit-eared bandicoot, is an Australian marsupial with long, skinny ears, large hind legs, and a bushy tail. A bulbul is one of a family of rather plain-looking Asian and African birds. Bulbuls are busy, noisy birds that grow up to 11 inches long.

Bilby

Bulbul

Can you get out of quicksand?

Yes, but not very easily. Quicksand looks solid, but will not support a person's weight. If you sink into quicksand, the first thing to do is not panic. Thrashing about will only make you sink deeper. By moving slowly and carefully, however, you can work your way to solid ground. You can also float on your back, the same as on water, until someone can pull you free.

Do wood-peckers get headaches?

TA-TA-TA-TA-TA-TA-TA!!

NOPE, I JUST GIVE THEM!

You might think so, but the answer is no. Big neck muscles support the woodpecker's extra-thick skull, which acts like a built-in crash helmet to absorb the force of its hammering blows. The woodpecker also has stiff tail feathers, which it presses against the tree for support, lessening the impact.

Why do some species of flower smell like rotting flesh?

P.U.!

SOMETHING SMELLS GOOD TO ME!

To attract flies. Plants such as the giant rafflesia, or "stinking corpse lily," rely on flies for pollination. The flowers' stinky smell ensures that plenty of flies show up to do the job.

How do pythons, boas, and other constrictor snakes kill their prey?

By squeezing them to death—but not by mashing them to a pulp. The snake wraps around its prey and squeezes a little tighter every time the prey breathes out. Eventually, the prey cannot breathe, and its heart stops.

What kind of bird lives underground and sometimes sounds like a rattlesnake?

BUZZ-Z-Z-Z-Z!

The burrowing owl. This bird makes its home in the abandoned burrows of prairie dogs or ground squirrels. When threatened in its nest, a young burrowing owl puts its vocal organ to work. It doesn't sing; it makes a buzzing sound similar to the warning sound of a rattlesnake, another animal often found in such holes. A predator will hesitate before charging in on what it thinks is a rattler!

Why don't European cuckoos build nests?

MAMA?

They don't need to. European cuckoos lay their eggs in the nests of other birds. A female cuckoo removes one of the nest owner's eggs, lays her own in its place, then leaves. The unsuspecting foster mother sits on it and, when it hatches, raises the baby cuckoo as its own.

DON'T FORGET ME ON MOTHER'S DAY!

Where do Suriname toads incubate their eggs?

In the female toad's back. The male fertilizes the eggs, then presses them into the female's back. Her skin covers the eggs until, after about 80 days, she sheds her skin. The tiny toads are set free into the water.

I COULD USE A REST—BUT THERE'S NEVER ANY SEAWEED AROUND WHEN YOU NEED IT!

Do sea horses swim the same way other fish do?

No. Unlike most fish, the sea horse swims in an upright position. It moves forward almost like a hummingbird, by flapping its tiny fins very fast—up to 35 times a second. Most fish use their tails to help them swim, but a sea horse uses its long, thin tail more like a hand than a fin. If a sea horse wants to stay in one spot for a while, it wraps its tail around seaweed or some other object and hangs on until it is ready to get going again.

Is there a reason why baby animals look so cute?

Scientists think that the big eyes of many baby animals let adult animals know that the youngsters are harmless and need care. Some baby animals have special markings, making adult animals less likely to chase them away, as they would if adult animals entered the same territory.

How do male silk moths find their mates?

I'M HERE, DEAR!

By smell, and very well, too. The female silk moth gives off a tiny, tiny amount of scent. Experiments show that just one molecule of this substance is enough to alert a male moth to her presence. He can find her from more than a mile away!

Why do eels travel to the Sargasso Sea?

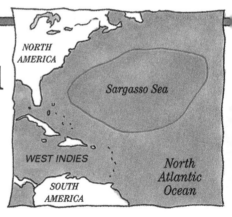

NORTH AMERICA

Sargasso Sea

WEST INDIES

SOUTH AMERICA

North Atlantic Ocean

To **spawn** (lay eggs). The Sargasso Sea is an oval-shaped area in the North Atlantic. European freshwater eels, using their sense of smell to guide them, travel thousands of miles across the sea back to the stretch of ocean where they were born in order to lay their own eggs.

THANKS FOR THE MAP. I'M ON MY WAY!

Why do birds sing?

To send other birds a message. Males do most of the singing. "This is my territory" seems to be the most common message. It may sound like a sweet song to us, but to other birds, it sounds like, "Keep out!"

For what animal were the Canary Islands named?

North Atlantic Ocean

AFRICA

CANARY ISLANDS

Dogs! The Latin word for dog is *canis*. Early explorers called the islands Canaria after the big, ferocious wild dogs they found living there. Canary birds, also found there, were named after the islands—not the other way around.

WHY ARE VULTURES GOOD TO HAVE AROUND?

Vultures are nature's clean-up crew. Experts believe that vultures living in Africa eat more meat than all other predators combined. Without vultures, rotting animal carcasses would spread disease, not to mention really stink things up!

What is the only kind of bird that can fly upside down?

The hummingbird—but not for long periods of time. Little hummers also fly backwards to pull their beaks out of flowers. Like helicopters, they fly up and down, hover, or zip away at speeds of more than 60 miles an hour. To do all this, hummingbirds flap their wings 50 to 75 times a second!

Do all tigers live in warm jungles?

No. The Siberian tiger, largest of all cats, lives in the Amur-Ussuri region of Siberia, Russia—not to mention northern China and Korea—which is covered with snow much of the year. To survive winter, the tiger grows an extra layer of fat.

How did guinea pigs get their name?

They were probably originally called Guiana (gee-AH-nuh) pigs because they make noises and movements that are a bit like those of regular pigs, and because Dutch traders found them in Dutch Guiana (now the independent country of Suriname), which is on South America's Caribbean coast. The animals' name eventually evolved into guinea pig.

Ducks are heavier than water, so why don't they sink?

Air trapped in ducks' feathers and held in their lungs makes them light enough to float. When a duck wants to dive under water for food, it exhales some air from its lungs to make it easier to sink. Waterproof feathers may also help ducks float.

Why do houseflies walk on food?

To find out what it tastes like. Houseflies have taste buds on their feet. If they like what they taste, they sponge saliva on the food until it dissolves, because flies can consume only liquids. Then they slurp it up!

Is there an obvious difference between centipedes and millipedes?

Centipede

Millipede

Yes, if you look closely. Centipedes have only one pair of legs on each body segment, except the last one. They can have as many as 170 segments, and have from 15 to 170 pairs of legs, depending on the number of body segments they have. Millipedes, on the other hand, have two pairs of legs per body segment, except for the first four. They have about 100 pairs of legs, with the actual number dependent on each insect's size.

Another difference is their diet: Centipedes eat other insects, while millipedes eat only plants.

Where and why do some people celebrate Buzzard Day?

In Hinckley, Ohio, the first Sunday after March 15 is Buzzard Day. Buzzard Day celebrates the return of migrating buzzards—actually, turkey vultures—that spend each summer near Hinckley. The first birds usually reach the area about March 15 each year.

Are Komodo dragons the kind of dragons found in fairy tales?

IF YOU KISS ME, I WON'T TURN INTO A PRINCE!

No. Komodo dragons are giant lizards that live on Komodo Island and a few other islands in Indonesia, in Asia. Komodo dragons can weigh up to 300 pounds and grow as long as 10 feet. They are so big that they can eat a wild goat whole! A Komodo dragon can live to be about 100 years old.

Why might you call the hognose snake and the opossum "animal actors"?

I'M PLAYING "DEAD."

When attacked, they often play dead, because most predators are likely to lose interest in unmoving prey and leave. The opossum lies on its side, usually refusing to move even if poked or prodded. The hognose snake rolls onto its back and lets its tongue fall out of its mouth. When the coast is clear, each "actor" wakes up and dashes off.

What makes the platypus an unusual mammal?

It lays eggs. Most mammals give birth to live young, except for monotremes. Monotremes are a rare group of animals with only three members: the platypus and two kinds of echidna (ih-KID-nuh), also called the spiny anteater. These animals are the only egg-laying mammals. (To make matters stranger, the platypus is also the only mammal with a duckbilled mouth.) Once eggs hatch, a monotreme mother provides her babies with milk, as other mammals do, but she doesn't have nipples. The babies suckle the milk as it oozes from her skin!

What is remarkable about the eyes of a giant squid?

Their size. Each eye measures 16 inches across—the size of an extra-large pizza! They are the biggest eyes in the world. But no one knows how well they can see.

I WISH I HAD A PIZZA!

DO OWLS NEED BRIGHT MOONLIGHT TO CATCH THEIR PREY?

No. In fact, barn owls can catch their prey in complete darkness, using their acute sense of hearing alone. Great gray owls can zero in on the sound of mice moving about in tunnels under the snow!

What strange thing happens to one eye of a baby flounder?

At first, a baby flounder has one eye on each side of its head, like every other fish. But as a flounder grows, one eye gradually moves across its head to the other side of its face. Eventually, both eyes are on the same side! The flounder spends its adult life lying on the ocean floor, eye side up.

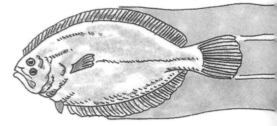

What does the four-eyed fish do with all those eyes?

I SEE YOU!

SO DO I!

It really has only two eyes, but each eye is divided into two parts. The fish lies just below the water's surface—half of each eye above water, half below. It hunts for food below, and keeps watch above for fish-eating seabirds. The four-eyed fish is also known as the anableps.

Why does a rabbit wiggle its nose?

I SMELL A CARROT!

To get a whiff of what is around it. Nose wiggling brings in air from many directions, enabling a rabbit to smell if any predators are around—or, if it is a pet rabbit, if its owner is carrying any carrots.

What kind of animals have their skeletons on the outside?

I'M THE MILLIPEDE.

I'M A BEETLE.

I'M A SPIDER.

I'M CRABBY!

Arthropods. This huge group includes insects, **arachnids** (spiders and scorpions), **crustaceans** (crabs, lobsters, and shrimps), and **myriapods** (centipedes and millipedes). Instead of having bones inside, arthropods have a hard outer surface called an exoskeleton. This shell supports and protects their squishy insides.

I'M THE CENTIPEDE.

Why don't birds fall off their perches when they sleep?

DO NOT DISTURB.

Leg locks. A bird bends its legs to perch. Bending the legs automatically pulls on muscles that make the bird's toes contract around its perch, holding the bird in place.

Why does a baby kangaroo depend on its mother's pouch?

A baby kangaroo, called a joey, is blind and helpless at birth, and weighs only a little more than a thumbtack. The joey crawls to its mother's pouch, where it finds warmth and food. It does not leave the pouch for about six months.

WOULD YOU LIKE TO HOP-ALONG WITH US?

What is an antlion?

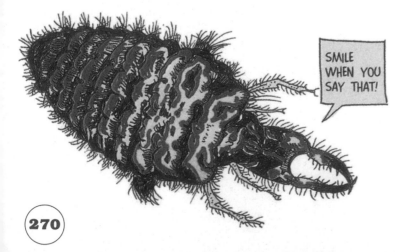

SMILE WHEN YOU SAY THAT!

The larva of a dragonfly-like insect, also known as a doodlebug. The antlion digs a cone-shaped pit into loose soil or sand, then hides at the bottom and waits for small insects to fall into the pit. While the insects struggle to climb up the steep, slippery sides of the pit to escape, the antlion snaps them up in its big jaws.

What are the hyrax's closest relatives?

You would never guess it by looking at one, but the hyrax is related to elephants and **dugongs** *(manatee-like sea mammals). The hyrax is a furry, rodentlike animal about the size of a rabbit. Hyraxes live in Africa and the Middle East.*

How can the toucan fly with such a big bill?

WANNA RACE?

The toucan's bill is large, but it is filled with air pockets, so it doesn't weigh much. Bright colors help the birds blend in among bright jungle colors. Thanks to its huge bill, a toucan can stand securely on a strong branch, reach for a piece of fruit, tilt its head, and gobble up its snack whole!

Which is smaller, a motmot or a mola-mola?

Definitely a motmot. The motmot is a long-tailed bird found in the forests of Central and South America. The largest are only about 20 inches long. The mola-mola, also called the ocean sunfish, is much larger. It can weigh 4,000 pounds and be 11 feet long!

Motmot

Mola-mola

What animal laid the largest eggs?

MAMA!

COMING, DARLING!

No, it wasn't a 100-foot-long dinosaur. The largest dinosaur eggs ever found are the size of cantaloupes. However, the moa—an extinct bird of New Zealand—laid eggs as big as watermelons!

Which dinosaur was most likely to flunk a test?

Scientists estimate a dinosaur's intelligence by comparing its brain size to its body size. Sauropods, such as *Diplodocus*, could be considered the least intelligent, because they had the smallest brains in relation to their body size. *Troodon*—which had a large brain in relation to its body size—may have been one of the smartest.

Where and when was the first complete dinosaur skeleton assembled and displayed?

Hadrosaurus foulkii (HAD-ruh-SORE-us FUL-kee-eye) was unearthed in New Jersey in 1858. It was the first skeleton found with enough bones to show what dinosaurs looked like. Ten years later, a mounted specimen was created from those bones and displayed at the Academy of Natural Sciences in Philadelphia.

Where did dinosaurs leave the tiniest fossil footprints?

The smallest known dinosaur footprints are in Nova Scotia, Canada. The inch-long tracks were made by a baby meat-eating dinosaur that was such a peewee, it would have fit in your hands.

HMMM!

Which dinosaur could be called a living fortress?

Animantarx was a nodosaur—a kind of ankylosaur—that had small horns on its cheeks and above its eyes. Ankylosaurs were heavily armored herbivores that are some-times called living tanks. *Animantarx*, which means "living fortress," was named in 1999.

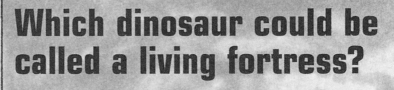

HMMM!

273

What good does a compost pile do?

Compost piles are made up of orange rinds, coffee grounds, eggshells, banana peels, leaves, grass, and other organic material. When these leftovers are mixed with soil for a few months, you wind up with a rich fertilizer. Besides being great for the garden, garbage that would otherwise wind up in a landfill goes back to the land instead.

Does radiation cause problems—or solve them?

Both. Radioactive waste products from nuclear power plants are a problem: If not disposed of carefully, they harm living things. Such waste must be sealed in special containers and buried or stored safely. Even so, many people fear that the radioactive waste might leak out and contaminate air, water, or soil.

However, radiation can also be helpful. For instance, doctors often use radioactive materials to kill cancer cells in patients.

SOME GOOD.

SOME BAD.

Is there pollution in space?

Yes. Traveling in space requires a lot of equipment. Space shuttles and satellites leave rocket boosters, empty fuel tanks, nuts, bolts, and paint chips in their wake. It can take many years for this space junk to hit Earth's atmosphere, where it will burn up. Each year, dozens of rockets are launched, which means that a lot of junk is left floating around.

WHAT IS HAZMAT?

Hazmat is short for "hazardous material." Hazmats are waste products created during the manufacture of many modern products, such as toys, clothes, computers, and cars. Some house-hold items—such as old paint cans, batteries, and weed killers—are also considered hazmats.

Do buildings ever get sick?

Yes. A building may be suspected of having sick building syndrome (SBS) when many people living or working in it start feeling ill at the same time. Symptoms may include headaches; irritation of the eyes, nose, and throat; nausea; and fatigue. Buildings with SBS usually have poor air circulation. Even worse, irritating chemicals may have become trapped in the air supply. To heal the building, experts must find and correct the problem.

What are some new uses for chicken feathers?

Scientists have figured out a way to make paper and plastic out of chicken feathers, which used to be considered garbage. Someday soon, the paper towels that you use to clean up a mess, the insulation in a house, and even the dashboard of a car may all be a little "fowl"!

How does global positioning work?

There are several global positioning system (GPS) satellites orbiting Earth. When a person turns on a GPS receiver, it receives signals from satellites that are within range. It then calculates where on Earth the user is—to within just 50 yards!

What do you get when you cross a jellyfish with a potato?

A potato that glows when it needs watering! Scientists have put jellyfish protein—which causes fluorescence, or glowing—in potato cells. When the potato needs water, it produces an acid that triggers the jellyfish protein, making the potato glow yellow. Monitors in the field spot the glow and send a signal that lets the farmer know that the plants need watering.

HURRY UP. I'M THIRSTY!

What is the difference between a CAT scan and a PET scan?

A CT (computerized tomography) or CAT scan machine takes a series of X-ray pictures that are like slices through the brain. A computer puts the images together to form a three-dimensional picture, allowing a doctor to look for very small differences in parts of the brain. PET (positron emission tomography) is like CT, except the patient gets a small shot of radioactive material first. This lets the doctor see what the brain is doing rather than just what shape it is in.

How will the HyperSoar aircraft fly?

By skipping along the top of Earth's atmosphere every 1,200 miles or so, just like a stone skipping across the water. The HyperSoar will be able to fly 10 times the speed of sound at an altitude of over 100,000 feet, covering the distance between San Francisco and Tokyo in about an hour and a half.

What is the difference between fog and smog?

Fog is a cloud that forms near the ground and stays low. It can occur at different times and last briefly or for a long time. Fog that forms in smoky air is called smog. Smog is often thicker than fog because smoke puts more particles in the air. Exhaust from vehicles and factories, and soot from fires, contribute to the smog that lies over major cities.

What is a monsoon?

A wind that reverses direction twice each year, causing two seasons, wet and dry. The heaviest rains that are part of the wet monsoon season fall in southern Asia and around the Indian Ocean. Cherrapunji, India, holds the record for the most rain in a single time period (192 inches in 15 days); the most in one month (366 inches); and the most in one year (1,042 inches)!

How fast can the wind . . . . . . blow?

A tornado that hit central Oklahoma on May 3, 1999, had the fastest wind ever measured on Earth: 318 miles per hour!

WHAT IS A WHITEOUT?

When a blizzard's combination of low cloud cover and falling snow make it impossible to see more than a few feet or even inches ahead. People who have been caught in a whiteout say that they couldn't tell the difference between the ground and the sky!

What is a dust devil?

Dust devils are whirlwinds caused by intense heating of dry ground, usually in desert areas. A rapid updraft of warm air starts a spin that can carry dust half a mile into the sky.

GOING UP!

279

What was the Cuban Missile Crisis?

For one week in October 1962, it seemed as if the Cold War between the Soviet Union and the United States was going to get very hot. U.S. spy planes had spotted Soviet nuclear-missile bases on communist-controlled Cuba, just 90 miles from Florida. President John F. Kennedy ordered a naval blockade of Cuba and put U.S. troops on alert. People everywhere were terrified, thinking that nuclear war could start at any moment. Finally, on October 28, the Soviets agreed to remove the nuclear weapons. The world breathed a sigh of relief.

What was unique about the Motown record label?

Motown was the first major label owned and operated by African Americans. It was started in 1959 by Berry Gordy Jr., a songwriter. Motown tunes topped hit charts through most of the 1960s. Unlike other "black music," Motown records were bought by both blacks and whites. Gordy ran his label like a film studio: The songs were written, arranged, and recorded all under the same roof. Motown's roster included the Four Tops, Smokey Robinson and the Miracles, Mary Wells, the Supremes, the Temptations, Stevie Wonder, and the Jackson Five.

What famous African-American leader told the world, "I have a dream"?

Dr. Martin Luther King Jr., noted civil-rights leader. On August 28, 1963, he led more than 200,000 peaceful demonstrators for equal rights on a march through Washington, D.C. It was the largest protest of its kind in the history of our nation's capital. King inspired the crowd—and people around the world—when he said, "I have a dream that one day this nation will rise up and live out the true meaning of its creed. 'We hold these truths to be self-evident, that all men are created equal.'"

When was U.S. President Kennedy assassinated?

On November 22, 1963. President John F. Kennedy and his wife, Jacqueline, were in Dallas, Texas, on a speaking tour. At 12:30 p.m., as they were riding in an open convertible in a motorcade, shots rang out. Kennedy slumped in the car's back seat as his horrified wife looked on. The 46-year-old president died 25 minutes later at Parkland Memorial Hospital. Vice President Lyndon B. Johnson was sworn in as president shortly thereafter.

Who were the Fab Four?

The Beatles, a hugely popular British rock 'n' roll group. When they first arrived in the U.S. on February 7, 1964, 25,000 fans greeted them at New York's Kennedy Airport. The pandemonium that followed John Lennon, Paul McCartney, George Harrison, and Ringo Starr wherever they went was known as Beatlemania. Sold-out concerts, huge record sales, and hit movies confirmed the Beatles' stardom. The band broke up in 1970, but its impact on popular music is still being felt today.

What was special about Walt Disney's 1928 cartoon, STEAMBOAT WILLIE?

HONK-HONK! TWEET! TOOT-TOOT!

It was the first cartoon to feature synchronized sound: characters that could speak, dance to music, and come to life with sound effects. The film starred a character named Mickey Mouse. Mickey's high-pitched voice was performed by one of his creators, Walt Disney. The cartoon was a success, and Disney's company went on to produce some of the most-loved animated films in history.

Whose 1927 film debut was called *Putting Pants on Phillip*?

Stan Laurel and Oliver Hardy—considered the most popular comedy duo in U.S. film history. They teamed up in 1926, after meeting in Hollywood. Audiences loved the duo's bumbling and bickering, and their sense of physical comedy. They starred in more than 60 short films and 27 feature films.

What were the LINDY HOP and the CHARLESTON?

Popular dances of the 1920s. The lindy hop began in New York City. Its name came from a dance fan who said, while watching a couple on the dance floor, "Look at those kids hoppin' over there. I guess they're doing the lindy hop!" "Lindy" was Charles Lindbergh, the pilot who had just made a historic transatlantic plane flight. The Charleston—developed in Charleston, South Carolina—was done with turned-in knees and turned-out toes and elbows at a frantic pace. It could be done alone, with a partner, or in a group.

WHO WERE THE MARX BROTHERS?

Chico Marx

A famous comedy team from New York City. Originally vaudeville stage performers, Chico, Harpo, Groucho, and Zeppo Marx released their first film, *The Cocoanuts*, in 1929. The brothers shot the film during the day, then performed their Broadway hit, *Animal Crackers*, on the stage at night! Their zany antics, wisecracks, and puns made them hugely popular (and fans still enjoy their films today). The Marx Brothers continued to make movies well into the 1940s.

Groucho Marx

Harpo Marx

Why is October 24, 1929, called Black Thursday?

During the 1920s, the U.S. economy grew rapidly. Many Americans invested money in the stock market, hoping to make a quick profit. But as the decade came to a close, the economy fell into serious trouble. On Saturday, October 19, share prices began to fall—and investors panicked. They sold their stocks at any price, and prices plummeted. On "Black Thursday," a record-high number of shares were traded. By the end of the week, people all over the world were facing financial ruin. The 1929 stock-market crash marked the beginning of the Great Depression of the 1930s.

How was PENICILLIN discovered?

By accident. Alexander Fleming, a Scottish bacteriologist, was trying to find a substance that would kill bacteria without harming humans. In 1928, he noticed that a bit of green mold growing in a culture plate had destroyed the bacteria around it! He isolated the active chemical in the mold, and named it *penicillin*. This nontoxic substance proved to be very effective against many bacteria harmful to people, such as those that cause pneumonia. Penicillin has saved untold millions of lives.

283

WHAT WAS THE JITTERBUG?

Which U.S. President was elected to office four times?

Franklin D. Roosevelt. He was the only U.S. president elected four times. FDR was first elected in 1932 during the Great Depression, and was reelected in 1936, 1940, and 1944. He died in office in 1945. In 1951, the states approved Amendment XXII to the Constitution, which limits the presidency to two terms.

What was the Holocaust?

It was a very popular dance. The jitterbug was first seen in the U.S. during the 1930s, but American soldiers stationed in Europe started a jitterbug craze in the 1940s. Female dancers wore swirling skirts, turned-down socks, and saddle shoes. The jitterbug was danced to swing music. Both partners had to be athletic to perform the "underarm swing."

The mass murder of European Jews and other groups by German Nazis during World War II. Nazi dictator Adolf Hitler planned to wipe out the entire Jewish population as part of his attempt to conquer the world. (The word *holocaust* has come to mean "widespread destruction.") Concentration and work camps were established to imprison Jews of all ages. Millions of Jews were killed in the camps and elsewhere. The Germans tried to keep their destructive actions a secret. But as the war came to end, Allied forces began to discover the camps—and the horrors of Hitler's plan.

When did the United Nations hold its first session?

On January 11, 1946, in London, England. Delegates from 51 countries discussed where the permanent headquarters should be located. (It was later agreed that it would be in New York City.) They also solved their first real problem—a conflict between Iran and the Soviet Union—by getting the two countries to settle their differences through negotiation, rather than war. The UN has worked toward world peace ever since.

WHAT WAS THE IRON CURTAIN?

"Iron curtain" was a phrase used by Britain's Sir Winston Churchill, in a 1946 speech, to describe the threat of communism. Churchill said that Europe was being divided by an "iron curtain": a split between democratic countries (such as Britain and France) and communist countries (led by the Soviet Union). He urged the U.S. and Britain to join efforts to discourage the spread of communism.

What piece of clothing caused a shock in 1946?

The bikini. It caused a sensation when it was first revealed in Paris, France, on July 5, 1946. The daring, tiny, two-piece swimsuit was created by a French designer, who named it after Bikini Atoll, a tiny island in the Pacific. (Four days earlier, an atom bomb had been tested on the island.) The name fit the swimsuit's "explosive" impact on the fashion world.

How did millions of gallons of oil pollute Alaska's shoreline?

On March 24, 1989, a large oil tanker called the *Exxon Valdez* ran aground in Alaska's Prince William Sound. Some 11 million gallons of oil spilled out, blackening hundreds of miles of coastline. Dead birds and fish began washing ashore, and Alaska's fishing industry suffered great losses. Exxon promised to clean up the area, but Alaska sued, charging the company with failing to adequately staff the tanker and supervise its crew.

How did nature delay the 1989 World Series?

At 5:04 p.m. on October 17, 1989, an earthquake struck San Francisco, where the San Francisco Giants and the Oakland Athletics were about to start the third game of the World Series. None of the 58,000 fans at Candlestick Park was seriously hurt, but city-wide about 90 people were killed and 3,000 were injured. The Bay Area suffered billions of dollars' worth of damage. The tremor, which measured 6.9 on the Richter scale, lasted 15 seconds. The Series resumed 10 days later at Candlestick Park. (Oakland won the Series in a four-game sweep.)

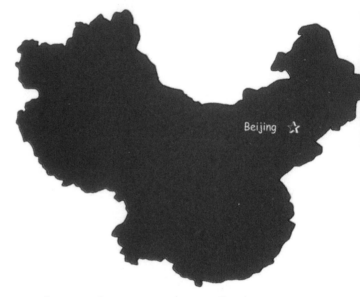

WHAT HAPPENED IN TIANANMEN SQUARE?

In the spring of 1989, students were holding pro-democracy demonstrations in Tiananmen Square in Beijing, China. China's government sent troops to break up the protest. On the morning of June 4, tanks rolled into the square and, sometime later, soldiers opened fire on the protesters. An estimated 5,000 people were killed and 10,000 injured. Outrage over the massacre was worldwide. Chinese authorities deny that it ever happened.

What famous "lady" celebrated her 100th birthday in 1986?

The Statue of Liberty—a gift from France that was dedicated on October 28, 1886. Americans celebrated Lady Liberty's 100th birthday on July 4, 1986. That day, despite temperatures in the 90s, long lines of people visited the newly restored Statue. Celebratory festivities included a parade of tall ships through New York Harbor and a huge fireworks display.

What was sold for the record-setting price of $53.9 million in 1987?

Irises, a painting by Vincent van Gogh (1853-1890). The art world was astounded when Alan Bond, an Australian businessman, paid that huge amount for a single painting. Van Gogh would have been, too: During his lifetime, he sold only one painting. But his popularity grew after his death. By the 1980s, museum exhibits of his vibrant, brightly colored paintings were drawing record-breaking crowds.

What symbolic divider was torn down in 1989?

The Berlin Wall *(below)*. That symbolic—and actual—barrier between East and West Berlin, in East Germany, came down in November 1989, as joyous crowds celebrated. Two years before, U.S. President Ronald Reagan and Soviet leader Mikhail Gorbachev had agreed to reduce the number of nuclear weapons aimed at one another's country, relaxing tensions between the Eastern and Western blocs. East and West Germany were reunited in 1990—after 41 years as two separate countries.

How many CURLS did child star Shirley Temple wear in her hair?

Fifty-six! Her mother, Gertrude, who made sure of the exact number, set them. At the 1935 Academy Awards ceremony, Shirley Temple, age 6, was awarded a miniature Oscar for her "outstanding contribution to screen entertainment" in 1934. That same year, she sang and danced in the films *The Little Colonel* and *The Littlest Rebel*. By the time Shirley was 10, she was the biggest box-office attraction in the nation.

Why did Britain's King Edward VIII give up his throne?

To marry Wallis Simpson, a divorced American. The king was under heavy pressure from the British government and church not to marry her. On December 11, 1936, in a radio broadcast that shocked his nation, Edward said that he was unable to bear the burden of being king without her. He gave the throne to his younger brother, George VI.

What did *Guernica*, Pablo Picasso's 1937 painting, depict?

Human terror and suffering when the town of Guernica, Spain, was bombed during the Spanish Civil War (1936-1939). It was the first time in history that a town or city was struck by an aerial bombing raid (1,700 people were killed). The painting was Picasso's protest against the destruction of the town by German bomber planes. The war in Spain was between army rebels (supported by Germany) and the elected government (supported by the Soviet Union). By the time resistance to the army collapsed, Spain was a devastated country.

What was the first recorded radio report to be broadcast coast to coast?

A report describing the explosion of the German dirigible *Hindenburg*, at Lakehurst, New Jersey, on May 6, 1937. An electrical storm approached as the ground crew struggled to moor the 804-foot, hydrogen-filled aircraft. There was a boom and a flash, then the *Hindenburg* exploded into flames. Thirty-five of the 97 people aboard were killed. A recording of broadcaster Herbert Morrison's description of the historic event was flown to New York, then broadcast nationwide.

WHO WAS JESSE OWENS?

An American track-and-field star of the 1936 Olympic Games. He won four gold medals at the Summer Games in Berlin, Germany. The excellence shown by Owens, an African American, embarrassed Germany's racist leader, Adolf Hitler. Hitler had expected his athletes to prove that Germans were the superior race. When this did not happen, he stormed out of the stadium, refusing to congratulate Owens.

What happened to Amelia Earhart?

She disappeared! Earhart and Fred Noonan, her navigator, were flying over the Pacific Ocean on the hardest leg of a round-the-world flight when their plane vanished near tiny Howland Island. On July 2, 1937, Earhart radioed the island, saying: "We are listening but cannot hear you." Earhart's last message, broadcast 45 minutes later, was unclear. The plane vanished, and she and Noonan were never seen again. Among the many achievements of the "first lady of the air" was becoming the first woman to fly solo across the Atlantic Ocean, in 1932.

In what movie was the expression "SUPERCALIFRAGILISTICEXPIALIDOCIOUS" sung?

Mary Poppins. This Disney musical comedy (1964) was adapted from P. L. Travers's children's stories about a nanny named Mary Poppins who has magical powers. It starred Julie Andrews as Mary and Dick Van Dyke as Bert, her chimney-sweep friend. *Mary Poppins* featured "Supercalifragilisticexpialidocious" and other memorable songs. The film, which combined live action with animation, won five Academy Awards.

When did the U.S. enter the conflict in Vietnam?

In March 1965, 3,500 U.S. Marines were sent to protect an air base at Da Nang, in South Vietnam. The base was being attacked by communist guerrilla troops known as the Vietcong. A year earlier, U.S. warplanes had begun bombing North Vietnam. By the end of 1965, a total of 250,000 U.S. troops had been sent to Vietnam. That year marked the beginning of U.S. involvement in a long and bloody war that continued until the U.S. withdrew in 1973. (U.S. involvement peaked in 1969, with 543,400 troops in Vietnam.)

Who was Indira Gandhi?

The first female prime minister of India. Her father, Jawaharlal Nehru, was India's first prime minister (1947-1964), after the country won independence from Great Britain. Indira Gandhi was elected its third prime minister in 1966, and held the office until 1977. In 1980, she was reelected to Parliament, and became prime minister for the second time. Gandhi's term was cut short in 1984, when she was assassinated by two of her security guards. Her son, Rajiv Gandhi, was elected prime minister in her place.

WAS *STAR TREK* AN INSTANT HIT WHEN IT PREMIERED ON TELEVISION?

When did the greatest power failure in history occur?

On November 9, 1965. Beginning at 5:16 p.m., the lights went out in the northeastern part of the U.S. and in two provinces of Canada! A switch failed at a power station near Niagara Falls, blacking out thousands of square miles and affecting 30 million people. Elevators stopped, traffic signals went out, hospital operating rooms went dark, and train passengers were stranded in tunnels and on bridges. In most areas, power was restored by the next morning.

no. It achieved only moderate success when it first aired on September 8, 1966. It may be hard to believe now, but in 1969, *Star Trek* was canceled! Outraged fans flooded the network offices with more than one million letters. *Star Trek* went on to achieve greater success in the following three decades than it did in its first run of 1966-1969. TV reruns, block-buster movies, magazines, books, and conventions all continue to fuel the *Star Trek* phenomenon.

WHERE DID THE WORD *VITAMIN* COME FROM?

In 1912, Polish biochemist Casimir Funk coined the term *vitamine*, meaning *essential to life*. Funk (who moved to the U.S. in 1915) used the word to describe essential factors contained in foods that were vital to the human body. (The *e* was later dropped.)

WHO WAS CALLED "THE GREATEST ATHLETE IN THE WORLD"?

Jim Thorpe, a Native American, was an outstanding college and professional football and baseball player. But it was at the 1912 Olympic Games in Stockholm, Sweden, where he earned this title. Thorpe became the first athlete to win both the pentathlon and the decathlon (track-and-field events). Sweden's king told Thorpe, "Sir, you are the greatest athlete in the world."

WHAT TWO OCEANS WERE LINKED IN 1913?

IT'S A PLEASURE TO MEET YOU!

HOW DO YOU DO!

The Atlantic and the Pacific. They were joined on October 9, 1913, when a dynamite explosion demolished the last barrier, allowing water to flow through the new Panama Canal. The first boat traveled through on January 7, 1914. A decade in the making, the canal eliminated the need for ships to travel around South America. The waterway shortened the sea voyage between New York City and San Francisco from more than 13,000 miles to fewer than 5,200.

WHO MADE ASSEMBLY-LINE MANUFACTURING A SUCCESS?

Henry Ford. His company used a system by which conveyor belts carried automobile parts to teams of workers. Each team performed a single task, such as adding or tightening a part. When that team finished, the auto was moved on to the next team. This resulted in much greater output and a big drop in price for consumers. Ford's method of assembly forever changed the way products are made.

WHO WAS CALLED "THE FUNNIEST MAN IN THE WORLD"?

IT WASN'T MY UNCLE HARRY!

Silent-film star Charlie Chaplin. His stardom began in 1914, when he first appeared as "The Little Tramp." This comical character wore a derby hat, a jacket that was much too small, and pants that were much too large. Movie audiences adored him. Chaplin was the director, producer, writer, and star of his hilarious films. He composed the music for his later movies, which had sound.

HOW DID HOLLYWOOD BECOME THE FILM CENTER OF THE WORLD?

The first motion-picture companies were based in New York City and Fort Lee, New Jersey. But the weather limited when and where they could film. Lured westward by California's year-round sun, filmmakers started shooting near a little town outside Los Angeles. The first Hollywood studio opened in 1911—and that once-sleepy town soon became "Tinsel Town," film capital of the world.

How many soldiers were found in the "Clay Army"?

Six thousand! The lifelike clay statues, lined up in battle formation, were discovered in July 1975. They were found under a three-acre burial mound in northwestern China. Experts believe that the figures were built during the reign of Emperor Shi Huangdi, from whom the name *China* is taken. His tomb and the clay warriors date from 210 to 203 B.C.!

Which Olympic athlete scored the first perfect "10"?

Nadia Comaneci. This tiny 14-year-old gymnast from Romania scored the first perfect "10" in gymnastics history. She scored 10 an amazing seven times at the 1976 Summer Games in Montreal, Canada. She won three individual gold medals: in the uneven parallel bars, balance beam, and all-around competitions. Barely 5 feet tall and only 83 pounds, Comaneci was the biggest star of the Montreal Olympics.

What is Legionnaires' disease?

A baffling and deadly virus. After an American Legion convention held in Philadelphia over the 1976 July 4th weekend, 221 Legionnaires became mysteriously ill. By the end of August, 29 were dead. Not until 1977 were scientists able to link the virus to the presence of bacteria in the drinking water. Today, Legionnaires' disease can be treated and prevented.

What two robots starred in a science-fiction movie?

R2D2 and C-3PO, in the 1977 blockbuster film *Star Wars*. This sci-fi movie, directed by George Lucas, used state-of-the-art technology to tell its classic story of good versus evil. Although there were exciting and dramatic moments among Luke Skywalker, Princess Leia, Han Solo, and Darth Vader, the funniest and most peculiar situations involved the robots.

Where was the world's first "test-tube baby" born?

The first baby conceived outside the human body was born in Manchester, England, on July 25, 1978. The healthy five-pound, twelve-ounce girl, named Louise, was born to Lesley and John Brown. Two British researchers, Dr. Robert Edwards and Patrick Steptoe, pioneered the "test-tube baby" technique, called in vitro fertilization. (*In vitro* is Latin for *in glass*.) One of Lesley Brown's eggs was fertilized in a test tube, then implanted in her womb to grow normally.

What special TV series drew 80 million viewers in 1977?

An eight-part drama called *Roots*. Its final two-hour episode, which aired on January 30, 1977, was seen by about 80 million viewers. Based on the book by Alex Haley, *Roots* traced the Haley family's history through the generations they lived as slaves in the American South, all the way back to an 18th-century ancestor abducted from West Africa.

WORLD WAR II

WHAT WAS THE BATTLE OF BRITAIN?

Germany's attempt to conquer Great Britain. German leader Adolf Hitler set off World War II by invading Poland in September 1939. In August 1940, the German air force began sending an average of 400 planes a day to bomb British airfields and towns. But the tiny Royal Air Force (RAF)—aided by radar, a new invention—valiantly defended the British Isles. That dashed Germany's hopes for a quick surrender, and Hitler had to abandon the idea of invading Britain.

How did the United States enter the war?

On December 7, 1941, Japan attacked and destroyed much of the U.S. Pacific fleet anchored at Pearl Harbor, Hawaii. The next day, the U.S. declared war on Japan. A few days later, Germany and Italy declared war on the U.S. The Allies (Great Britain, Canada, Australia, New Zealand, France, China, the Soviet Union, and the U.S.) were then at war with the Axis Powers (Germany, Japan, and Italy). In all, World War II involved 40 countries and almost 70 million soldiers.

Who was "Rosie the Riveter"?

"Rosie" was not a real person, but a symbolic name for all the U.S. women who went to work—many for the first time—while the men were at war. Women became expert welders, truck drivers, and crane operators and did many other jobs once done only by men. Female factory and shipyard workers helped the country through a difficult time.

How long did the siege of Leningrad last?

For 900 days. Starting in September 1941, German troops tried to starve the people of the Soviet Union's second-largest city into surrendering. At least 641,000 Leningrad residents died of hunger, illness, or the cold, but the Soviets refused to surrender their city. The siege ended in January 1944, when Red Army forces reached Leningrad and drove the Germans away.

What was Operation Overlord?

"Operation Overlord" was the code name for the largest sea-borne invasion in history. On June 6, 1944—D-Day—a fleet of ships dropped some 175,000 Allied soldiers on the beaches of Normandy, France. Though taken by surprise, the Germans fiercely defended the fortified coast. But by the end of August, the victorious Allies had liberated Paris.

How did the Manhattan Project end the war with Japan?

"Manhattan Project" was the name of a secret project in which a team of scientists developed an atom bomb in the U.S. The first time their creation was ever used in war was on August 6, 1945, when a U.S. bomber dropped one on Hiroshima, Japan. It killed about 80,000 people. Days later, a second atom bomb devastated the city of Nagasaki, Japan, killing more than 65,000 people. Japan officially surrendered on September 2, 1945.

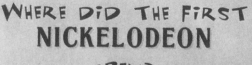

WHERE DID THE FIRST NICKELODEON OPEN?

I HOPE I DON'T SIT IN BACK OF HER.

NOW SHOWING

In Pittsburgh, Pennsylvania, in 1905. Usually, nickelodeons were stores that owners converted into movie theaters by installing chairs. A pianist played music that fit the action on the silent screen. These theaters were called nickelodeons because the admission fee was five cents.

WHAT WAS THE FIRST COUNTRY TO ALLOW FEMALE CITIZENS TO VOTE?

Finland granted women the vote in 1906, while it was still under Russian rule. The first fully independent country to grant equal voting rights was Norway, in 1913. The struggle for suffrage (voting rights for women) had begun at the first Women's Rights Convention in Seneca Falls, New York, in 1848. By 1900, that right had been won in several U.S. states and in New Zealand (then part of the British Empire). Not until 1920, when the 19th Amendment to the Constitution was passed, could U.S. women vote nationwide.

WHAT STARTED A THREE-DAY FIRE THAT DEVASTATED SAN FRANCISCO?

A severe earthquake. A few terrifying days in April 1906 were all it took to turn much of that thriving city into rubble. Thousands of panicked citizens fled. Others gathered in public squares and parks for safety. Damage estimates ran as high as $250 million. It was the worst disaster California had ever experienced.

WHO BECAME THE FIRST AFRICAN-AMERICAN HEAVYWEIGHT BOXING CHAMPION?

Jack Johnson of Galveston, Texas. He won by a TKO (technical knockout) on December 26, 1908, in Sydney, Australia. Although many white people were unhappy about a black man being boxing's champion, Johnson retained his title until 1915. He retired from the ring in 1928, after 112 professional bouts. He later appeared in vaudeville and carnival acts, and wrote two books about his life.

HOW WAS CELLOPHANE DISCOVERED?

By accident! A Swiss chemist named Jacques E. Brandenberger did it in 1908. Hoping to invent a stain-resistant tablecloth, he sprayed viscose on cloth. (Viscose is a thick, golden-brown solution taken from a plant fiber called cellulose.) Brandenberger found that he could peel the coating from the tablecloth in a thin, see-through sheet. Instead of inventing one useful household item, he had discovered another!

WHEN WAS THE FIRST MODEL T FORD BUILT?

The first Model T rolled off the production line in Detroit, Michigan, on August 12, 1908. Henry Ford, founder of the Ford Motor Company, wanted to build a strong and sturdy car. So he made it out of a tough, lightweight, steel alloy. He also wanted his cars to be affordable for most families, so he used a production line, to make them quickly and cheaply. At $850, Ford's Model T—fondly known as the Tin Lizzie—was an instant success.

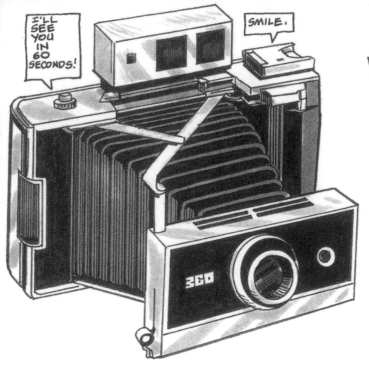

Who developed the first instant camera?

Edwin Land, founder and president of the Polaroid Corporation. In 1947, he demonstrated the first instant camera. It took black-and-white pictures that developed into prints in only 60 seconds! By the 1970s, Land had improved the Polaroid camera to take and develop color pictures within 50 seconds.

What did scientist Percy Spencer discover by accident?

Microwave cooking. While working in a lab, Spencer noticed that a candy bar in his pocket had melted. He figured out that the microwave signals he had been using in the lab had caused the candy bar's molecules to vibrate rapidly. This caused friction among the molecules, which created heat, which melted the candy bar. The first microwave oven was patented in 1945.

WHEN WERE LONG-PLAYING RECORDS INTRODUCED?

In 1948. Before then, most records were made of a shellac-and-clay mixture and were played on a phonograph at 78 rpm (revolutions per minute). They broke easily, and could hold only four minutes of music per side. In 1948, Columbia Records developed a 33 1/3-rpm, long-playing (LP) record made of vinyl. LPs held nearly 25 minutes of music per side, provided better sound quality, and were more durable. The vinyl LP was the standard for decades—until the arrival of cassette tapes (1963) and compact discs (1982).

Who was the first baseball player to earn $100,000 a year?

Centerfielder Joe DiMaggio, in 1949. Many people criticized his big contract request, but DiMaggio was invaluable to his team, the New York Yankees. He was voted the American League's MVP (Most Valuable Player) in 1939, 1941, and 1947. In 1941, he set the hitting-streak record by hitting safely in 56 consecutive games! DiMaggio, who played his entire career (1936-1951) with New York, was nicknamed "the Yankee Clipper" for the classy, determined, and graceful way he played the game.

When was Silly Putty™ invented?

During World War II, when James Wright, a General Electric engineer, was trying to develop a substitute for rubber. He came up with a substance that could be bounced and stretched. For his purposes, however, it was a failure: It stretched far more than natural rubber, and would not keep its form. It was fun to play with, though, so he kept it around. It later became a popular toy.

WHO FOUNDED THE PEOPLE'S REPUBLIC OF CHINA?

Mao Zedong. He led the long struggle against Chiang Kai-shek for control of China. Mao proclaimed the People's Republic in October 1949. As chairman of China's Communist Party, he controlled the nation's artistic, military, industrial, and agricultural policies. Mao gave up his title in 1959, but kept control of the country until his death in 1976.

Where did the Battle of Wounded Knee take place?

WOUNDED KNEE

AIM

The last major battle between the U.S. cavalry and Native Americans took place in 1890 at Wounded Knee, South Dakota. But on February 27, 1973, members of the American Indian Movement (AIM) held a protest at the Pine Ridge Sioux Reservation in Wounded Knee. They took over a trading post and church, and demanded that the U.S. Senate investigate the government's unfair treatment of Indians. The "new" Battle at Wounded Knee—a 70-day standoff with FBI agents—resulted in two deaths, many injuries, and more than 300 arrests.

How did people deal with the mid-1970s gasoline shortage?

NO GAS TODAY

PUSH!

In 1973, an embargo (ban) on oil shipments to the U.S. forced many gas stations to close for lack of gas. Open stations had lines miles long! In some places, sales were limited to $2 or $3 per car. In others, people with odd-numbered license plates could buy gas on odd-numbered days, while people with even-numbered plates did so on even-numbered days. Things got easier in April 1974, when the embargo was lifted.

Who broke Babe Ruth's career home-run record?

OUCH! THAT'S 715!

I GOT IT!

Henry (Hank) Aaron. He made baseball history on April 8, 1974. Aaron entered that day's game tied with Babe Ruth's 39-year-old record of 714 career home runs. At his second at-bat, "Hammerin' Hank" slammed a fastball over the outfield fence! Fireworks went off and the hometown crowd in Atlanta, Georgia, went wild. By the time Aaron retired in 1976, he had set a new career-homers record: 755.

Who was the first U.S. president to resign?

Richard M. Nixon. He announced his resignation on August 8, 1974, because Congress was about to impeach him (charge him with wrongdoing) for his part in a scandal known as Watergate. Nixon's troubles began in 1972, when five men were caught bugging the Democratic Party's election-campaign headquarters. The investigation that followed exposed President Nixon as being involved in covering up illegal acts by his aides.

In what country were the "killing fields"?

Cambodia. In 1975, the country in southeast Asia, was taken over by a communist group called the Khmer Rouge. This regime, led by a man named Pol Pot, terrorized the Cambodian people. Educated or professional people were murdered. City dwellers were taken into the countryside and forced to work as farmers; many starved to death while laboring in the fields. At least one million Cambodians lost their lives in what came to be known as "the killing fields."

HOW DID ARTHUR ASHE ACHIEVE GREATNESS?

On July 5, 1975, Ashe beat tennis star Jimmy Connors in an exciting four-set final to win the Wimbledon singles championship in England. He was the first African-American male player to win at Wimbledon. Ashe was no stranger to success. In 1968, he had won the U.S. Open and played on the U.S. Davis Cup team. In 1970, he won the Australian Open. Ashe retired in 1980 and became a writer and an activist for racial and social justice.

WHERE DID THAT COME FROM?

WHO LAUNCHED THE FIRST ARTIFICIAL SATELLITE?

The Soviet Union astonished the world when it launched *Sputnik I* on October 4, 1957. At 184 pounds, it was many times heavier than the satellite the U.S. launched the following year. *Sputnik I* circled Earth once every 96 minutes for 92 days, sending back radio signals. Today, many weather, military, communications, and scientific satellites orbit Earth.

WHAT WERE TWO OF THE MOST POPULAR TOYS DURING THE 1950s?

The Frisbee® and the hula hoop. In 1957, an executive from the Wham-O® toy company noticed college students twirling pie tins through the air—tins that were made by the Frisbie Pie Company (Wham-O® adapted the name). The popular Frisbee® is still being tossed around today. The following year, Wham-O® introduced the plastic hula hoop, and twenty million were sold in less than a year!!

Were drive-in movie theaters common in the '50s?

I SAW THIS LAST NIGHT.

Yes! The first drive-in opened in Camden, New Jersey, in 1933. But it was not until the 1950s, when more Americans could afford cars, that the outdoor theaters' popularity exploded. Curved rows of parked cars, each with a small speaker placed inside, faced a large screen. Some drive-ins even supplied heaters during the winter months. By the end of the 1950s, there were more than 4,000 drive-ins in the U.S.

Who were the first seven astronauts chosen by NASA?

Scott **C**arpenter, **G**ordon **C**ooper, **J**ohn **G**lenn, **G**us **G**rissom, **W**alter **S**chirra, **A**lan **S**hepard Jr., and **D**eke **S**layton. They were chosen out of more than 500 candidates as the first American astronauts. This group, selected in April 1959, was made up of Air Force, Navy, and Marine Corps test pilots. The National Aeronautics and Space Administration (NASA) had great plans for them in the approaching decade.

What does the phrase "the day the music died" refer to?

February 3, 1959. On that day, a plane crash took the lives of three popular rock 'n' roll performers. Buddy Holly *(right)*, Ritchie Valens, and J. P. "Big Bopper" Richardson had played a sold-out show in Mason City, Iowa. Instead of taking a bus to the next stop on their tour, they took a single-engine aircraft, which crashed in a snowstorm.

WHAT WAS THE QUIZ SHOW SCANDAL?

In November 1959, TV's most popular quiz show, *Twenty-One*, was revealed as a fake! A contestant named Charles Van Doren, who had won $129,000, admitted that he had been given the answers to difficult questions in advance. *Twenty-One*'s producer testified before Congress that the goal of the deception was to create excitement and to boost ratings. Soon other quiz and game shows were accused of cheating. The scandal led to the FCC (Federal Communications Commission) setting new standards for TV broadcasters.

GLENN   COOPER   CARPENTER   SHEPARD   SCHIRRA   GRISSOM   SLAYTON

What was the major source of home entertainment in the 1930s?

Radio. In the evenings, families gathered in their living rooms to listen to comedies and dramas. Popular programs, such as *The Shadow*, *Dick Tracy*, and *The Lone Ranger*, kept people glued to their radios. Concerts and other music programs were also popular—so popular that the term *disc jockey* was coined to describe radio announcers who played records. In the late 1930s, as another major war seemed likely, radio stations developed news departments to report on the latest events in Europe.

What pre-Halloween radio program made Americans panic?

On October 30, 1938, actor-producer Orson Welles broadcast a science-fiction thriller entitled "Invasion from Mars." The sound effects were so good that millions of radio listeners thought it was the real thing! Welles's radio play (based on the book *War of the Worlds* by H. G. Wells) sounded like a news broadcast about Martians invading New Jersey. It sounded so real that hundreds of people ran out of their homes with handkerchiefs over their mouths to guard against "Martian gas"!

Where did "CRYSTAL NIGHT" take place?

In Germany and Austria. On the night of November 9, 1938, Adolf Hitler's Nazi troops broke into and wrecked thousands of stores run by Jewish merchants. Jews were attacked and beaten, and hundreds of Jewish homes and places of worship were set on fire. That outburst of violence became known as *Kristallnacht*—"the night of broken glass"—because of the piles of broken glass from smashed store windows left in the streets.

Who was the first U.S. president to appear on TV?

Franklin D. Roosevelt. On April 30, 1939, television cameras filmed the speech he gave at opening-day ceremonies for the World's Fair held in Queens, a borough of New York City. The crude TV pictures were fuzzy but recognizable. Development of this new medium was temporarily halted when World War II broke out in Europe four months later.

What comic book character was created by 18-year-old artist Bob Kane?

Batman. Kane originally called his superhero Birdman, but by the time the Caped Crusader appeared in the May 1939 issue of *Detective Comics*, his name had been changed. Kane was one of the first illustrators to use movie-style angles in comics, creating an eerie, shadowy atmosphere. Since 1939, Kane's character has appeared in radio programs, television series, and many movies.

WHAT $3,000,000 MUSICAL FILM FANTASY PREMIERED ON AUGUST 15, 1939?

The Wizard of Oz. Based on a 1900 novel by L. Frank Baum, this classic story had already been made into movies, short cartoons, a stage show, and a radio program. But the 1939 film version, starring Judy Garland as Dorothy, is the most famous. The MGM studio spent an extra $250,000 to promote what it called "the greatest picture in the history of entertainment."

HIGH-TECH TIMES

What is the World Wide Web?

A key feature of the Internet—a vast network of computers that connects businesses, institutions, and individuals. Anyone with a computer and modem can connect to the Web. The World Wide Web provides information on a vast array of topics, along with sound, pictures, and video. Users can also communicate with one another by e-mail.

What was unique about the movie *Toy Story*?

It was the first movie created entirely on computer. Pixar Animation Studios used the latest, most sophisticated technology available to create dazzling effects and realistic detail for the 1996 Disney hit. The only thing "human" in the movie were the characters' voices, supplied by an all-star cast of actors including Tom Hanks, Tim Allen, and Don Rickles.

How is virtual reality used?

Virtual reality (VR) technology was first developed in the 1960s as flight simulators, to help train pilots. NASA and the U.S. military developed it further, improving computer imagery. By the 1990s, VR was being used to train U.S. troops and astronauts, as well as medical students studying surgery and other medical techniques. VR also became popular in computer and video games and other fields of entertainment. Engineers, architects, advertisers, and workers in many other fields have found it useful, too.

When will the first international space station be finished?

By the year 2010—if all goes according to plan. The first parts for the station, known as *Alpha* (which means *first*), were flown into space in November 1998. An estimated 88 such flights will be needed to complete the job. The project is being organized and paid for by the U.S., Canada, Russia, Japan, Brazil, and 11 European nations. When finished, the "city in space" will provide a permanent orbiting research complex for scientists, engineers, and entrepreneurs.

What was the first animal ever cloned?

THAT'S US!!

A female sheep named Dolly. A clone is a genetically identical copy of a living organism. Dolly, born in July 1996, was the first mammal ever created from the nonreproductive tissue of an adult animal. Dr. Ian Wilmut and a team of scientists in Edinburgh, Scotland, took a normal embryo (egg) cell from an adult sheep and removed its nucleus (which contains the genetic material). Then they took a cell from another sheep's mammary gland and fused it to the emptied cell. In other words, they grew an animal from scratch!

How did technological advances change communications in the 1990s?

New technologies enabled people to communicate over great distances faster and more easily than ever. Telephones went wireless, then got smaller, lighter, and more powerful. So did computers. Satellites linked vast communications networks together, so that any one communications device (phone, computer, fax machine) could "talk" and send pictures to another, anywhere in the world. This created a whole new way of working: telecommuting. Telecommunication enables workers to take part in meetings, treat patients, supply clients, and provide other types of services to people hundreds or thousands of miles away.

Index

Who was Sitting Bull? • What makes rainbows appear? • **What is virtual reality?**

How do you travel light? • Who were the Maya? • **What's at the center of Earth?**

Who was Mozart? • Is a four-leaf clover lucky? • **Why do monkeys groom each other?**

Do vampires really exist? • What are robots used for? • **Do animals use tools?**

What causes twins? • **Who was Harry Houdini?** • Are all sharks dangerous?

Who was Jackie Robinson? • **What is a meteor?** • Who was Queen Elizabeth I?

How do plants eat? • **How do spiders spin webs?** • What is a vaccine?

When was the first car invented? • **How does an electric guitar work?**